ROOM FOR RENT

ROOM FOR RENT

Anton J. S. Keating, Esq.

JUGGLING JUSTICE
PRESS

Copyright © 2018 Anton J.S. Keating

ISBN 13: 978-0-692-12979-1
ISBN 10: 0692129790

All rights reserved. No part of this publication may be reproduced, distributed, or transmitted in any form or by any means, including photocopying, recording, or other electronic or mechanical methods, without the prior written permission of the publisher, except in brief quotations embodied in critical reviews and certain other noncommercial uses permitted by copyright law. For permission requests, write the author at the address below:

Anton J.S. Keating
614 Colorado Avenue
Baltimore, Maryland 21210

Learn about Keating's other book, *I'm Not Really Guilty*, detailing his role as the defense attorney in the longest murder trial in Maryland's history, at www.imnotreallyguilty.com.

First Edition

Printed in the United States of America

Contents

Acknowledgments i
Preface iii
Introduction v
Chapter 1: The Murder of Doris Martin 1
Chapter 2: Keating Defends Smith 20
Chapter 3: Smith's Criminal History 35
Chapter 4: In Court—First Appearance 38
Chapter 5: Smith Psychological Profile, Family &
  Personal History 66
Chapter 6: Smith's Criminal History—The Recidivist 73
Chapter 7: A Glimpse into Smith's Prison Life 81
Chapter 8: The Trial, Part I 88
Chapter 9: The Trial, Part II 103
Chapter 10: The Appeal 109
Chapter 11: Lady Justice Weighs In 115
Epilogue 128
Excerpt from *Lara* by Lord Byron 130
Appendix A: Chronology 133
Appendix B: Letter Re Criminal Charges Against
  Smith in Virginia 140
Appendix C: Victim Impact Statements from
  Sacramento, California 146

Acknowledgments

I wish to thank the following people for their work writing, editing, and designing this book: The Honorable Darcy Rood, Kim Ledgerwood, Aliza Worthington, Elizabeth Gething, Mari Christie, and Ellie Sipila. Without their active participation and encouragement, this book would never have been completed.

—Anton J. S. Keating

Preface

Throughout my career as a prosecutor and defense attorney in the city of Baltimore, I prosecuted and defended scores of murder cases. I became accustomed to the question that inevitably followed when I told someone I was a public defender, "How can you defend a murderer?"

I always answered, "Very well."

This was, of course, in stark contrast to the stock response from defense counsel that they are protecting constitutional rights. To my mind, there really is nothing noble about it.

Given my adversarial nature, I can easily admit—after a drink or two—that I wasn't moved to fight for this abstract constitutional principle. The truth is that I fight only because I like to fight. Righteousness has no role in my actions—I just want to win.

I inherited "the fighting disease" from my father—a condition, he advised, that afflicts many an Irishman. My father was a retired boxer and my older brother and I were "in training" from the day we could walk. Family photos show me in a proper boxing stance, even as a toddler. My father saw my brother and me as sparring partners. (This approach to child rearing does not really promote sibling harmony, if you happen to be wondering.) Yet, I learned early on that I didn't have the desire or the talent to follow my father and pursue a boxing career.

I did, however, have his disease: I love to fight. Law provided a respectable vehicle for me to pursue this passion.

INTRODUCTION

James Francis Smith was a cunning sociopath who spent more than 40 years victimizing older, vulnerable women. He used an elaborate, well-thought-out con to take advantage of countless victims, preying on their trusting natures. Most of the time, he just robbed these women, but sometimes he raped or murdered them as well.

Smith was caught and incarcerated repeatedly throughout his life, but he was a master manipulator who maneuvered his way through the "justice" system and secured his release over and over again. Laws that are put in place to protect the innocent often protect the guilty.

It's commonly proclaimed in the legal field that it is better for 100 guilty people to go free than for one innocent man to be imprisoned.

True enough.

But, sometimes, it just doesn't feel that simple.

Chapter 1:
The Murder of Doris Martin

On November 13, 1973, the residents of the 3400 block of Chestnut Avenue were growing concerned. They hadn't seen their neighbor Doris Martin since the day before. Martin was 65 years old, and she had lived almost her entire life in her Hampden row home. Well known and well liked among her long-time neighbors, Martin had never married and never been employed. She spent many years caring for her ailing grandparents and her parents. Now, she lived alone except for her precious companion—her toy poodle, Buffy.

Although her house was a block away from the North District Police Station, Martin had come to fear her neighborhood because it had become a high crime area. Nevertheless, she took Buffy for a walk around the neighborhood every morning without fail. When she missed her routine, the neighbors noticed and worried.

They had last seen Martin around 6 p.m. the previous day, when she walked to a nearby store. Three residents from the Hampden neighborhood—Esther Arnold, Doris Crouse, and Rose Piper—eventually decided to check Martin's home to see if she was okay. They got no response when they knocked, so Arnold brought her ladder over, and the women put it up against Martin's row home, securing entry through a second-floor window. Crouse entered the home, walked downstairs, opened the rear kitchen door, and let her neighbors inside.

It was then that Piper went upstairs and discovered blankets covering something on the bed in a second-floor bedroom. The blankets were sticking to whatever lay underneath, and Piper was too nervous to explore further. Distraught, the neighbors immediately called the police.

Officer Slawinski was nearby on routine patrol and arrived at the crime scene within minutes of the 911 call. He discovered Martin's body, lying dead, underneath two blankets: a brown wool blanket covered her from the waist down, and a pink blanket covered her head. Martin's pantyhose were pulled halfway down her buttocks, her hands were tied, and her arms were at unnatural angles behind her back. There was blood splattered all over the room: on the head of the bed, the night table, a chair in the southwest corner, a bureau against the south wall, and the curtains hanging against the west wall. It was a gruesome scene.

Slawinski called in the Homicide Unit, requesting both a mobile crime lab unit and a morgue wagon. He pronounced Doris Martin dead at 2:40 p.m.

Martin was a well-liked woman who never bothered anyone and devoted most of her energy to her ailing dog. According to the neighbors, she rarely slept in her bedroom, the room where her body was found. Instead, she frequently slept downstairs near Buffy, so she could attend to the dog's recurring asthma attacks. Martin had even recently purchased a new air conditioner to relieve the dog's asthma. While the neighbors and Slawinski were on the scene, Buffy stood barking at the top of the stairs. She refused to leave her owner's side.

John Sloan, Martin's attorney, also arrived at the crime scene. He told the police that Martin had rented out rooms for more than 15 years but had not taken in any boarders for the last two years because of the recent crime in the area. She had recently become distressed about her finances, however, and felt she had no choice but to resume renting rooms in her home despite the risks.

Hesitant, she had placed her first ad in the newspaper on the previous Sunday, November 11. Martin told a neighbor she had received two calls that very night. The first call was from a man in Dundalk, Maryland, who asked for her address but later phoned to say he was no longer interested. The second call was from an unknown man who said he'd come by and see the room the next day.

Detective Sergeant William Kearney and Detective James Russell of the homicide squad arrived on the crime scene at 3:30 p.m. Russell was a young officer, on the job for six years. He summoned an assistant city medical examiner for an on-the-scene determination of the cause of death and directed the crime lab to photograph both the inside and outside of the home. He also directed other crime lab officers to dust for fingerprints in the room where the murder occurred, as well as all the other rooms in the home, paying particular attention to the kitchen, where one of the drawers had been left open.

An immediate search for the murder weapon was conducted in the house, garden, and alley behind the house, with no success. (Russell returned a month later to search for additional evidence. His efforts were rewarded when he found a brick up against the door to the entrance of the kitchen. The brick appeared to have blood and some other type of matter on it, but it did not contain any fingerprints.)

Russell carefully supervised the taking of the photographs and the scrapings of the sprays of blood on the ceiling and walls of the bedroom for blood-type categorization. In the entire house, only three possible latent fingerprints were found.

Martin's nostrils contained two tiny pieces of tissue paper, and tissue paper and a face cloth covered in human blood were also found in the bathroom. Russell examined the living room and discovered a table near the front door. On it, there was a set of house keys, a telephone, and a piece of note paper with writing on it. Russell looked at the note carefully. (He later submitted it to the FBI Crime Lab in Washington, D.C., along with samples of Martin's handwriting, and the FBI determined that the note was, in fact, in Martin's handwriting.)

Detective Frank Perkowski of the Criminal Investigation Homicide Unit was put in charge of the investigation, along with Kearney and Russell. They soon switched into high gear.

Martin's house was a two-story row home located in Hampden, a low-income, white area of Baltimore. There were no signs of forced entry to either entrance of the house and all the windows were locked, with the exception of one leading to the first-floor bathroom on the south side of the house. This was the window that had been forced open by the neighbors who discovered Martin's body. Additionally, her front door had a deadbolt lock that could only be locked with a key. The door was closed and locked, indicating that the assailant had left by the rear door. Martin's door keys were the ones on the table in the living room, and they were taken into evidence. The rear door was equipped with a night-latch lock, which enabled the door to be locked without a key. This particular door was also observed to be closed and locked.

Russell searched the entire premises and observed that the rooms appeared to have been searched. Most obviously, the kitchen appeared to have been ransacked, indicating a possible robbery motive by the unknown perpetrator. The main piece of evidence gathered from the scene was the note Russell discovered on the table in the living room. On one side of the note was the following information[1]:

---

1. The notes from Martin are transcribed verbatim here.

I have some one coming to see the room tomorrow morning and he has asked me to save it for him. But I have to *see* the *man* and *talk* to him *first*. Could you please give me a call in the morning around noon or could I call you?

The reverse side of the note had some numbers scrawled on it and read: *Cuffington, 4, Pittsburg, H.J Hines, 2.*

State of Maryland, Department of Health and Mental Hygiene, Medical Examiner's Certificate of Death, indicating Martin was beaten and stabbed by an assailant. 1973.

Assistant Medical Examiner Dr. Craig Duncan and Dr. Irvin Sopher from the Office of the Chief Medical Examiner arrived at 6 p.m. and found that Martin had been struck at least once on the head with a blunt object and stabbed several times in the back. At the time, Duncan stated that he thought Martin had been dead for approximately 18 hours and set the time of death for the evening hours of November 12. He observed the position of the body, the blood stains, and the spattering of the walls and furniture and concluded that Martin had sustained a severe blow to the head while she was face down on the bed where her body had been discovered.

While on the scene, Slawinski interviewed Mrs. Mann, a neighbor and close friend of Martin's. She relayed that she had spoken to Martin on the telephone around 4 p.m. on November

12, and Martin told her that she had rented a room to a man who worked for H.J. Heinz Company and had recently been transferred to Baltimore City. The man also informed Martin that another man would be coming to her house later in the evening to deliver his trunk from Pittsburgh, Pennsylvania.

On November 14, the Office of the Chief Medical Examiner performed the post-mortem examination. Martin's blood type was identified as A positive. Martin had sustained a head injury, which was evidenced by a large laceration (4 inches by one-half inch) to the right side of the head and two smaller scalp lacerations. Underlying the lacerations, there was a major fracture of the skull and a brain injury. There was also bruising and a loosening of the lower teeth compatible with a blow to the face. In addition, Martin sustained seven stab wounds to the lower left back, four of which were very deep, penetrating the left lung, causing hemorrhaging.

Duncan was of the opinion that the cause of death was the totality of the four deep stab wounds and blunt force injury to the head, resulting in the skull fracture. Either the stab wounds or the head injuries alone would have been enough to cause death. While there was no evidence Martin had been sexually molested, crime lab photos clearly showed that her pantyhose were pulled down. The time of death was narrowed down to sometime between 5:30 p.m. on November 12 and 5:30 a.m., November 13. The official cause of death was listed as "cranio-cerebral injuries and multiple stab wounds of back."

The next, day, November 15, Detective Walter Egger of the Criminal Investigation Homicide Unit contacted Perkowski with an interesting development. The week before, Egger's grandfather, Anthony Hagerman, had placed an ad in *The Baltimore Sun* to rent a room at his house. Hagerman received a telephone inquiry from a man about the room, but when Hagerman questioned him, the man refused to provide any information and hung up. Hagerman placed this same ad with *The Baltimore Sun* newspaper again on November 11, 1973. At about 9 p.m. on November 12, Hagerman received another telephone inquiry about the room from a male that identified himself as a Mr.

Hutzler of the H.J. Heinz Company of Pittsburgh, Pennsylvania. Hagerman told the man he could visit the home on November 13 if he was interested in the room, but the caller didn't keep this appointment. Hagerman's grandson requested that he continue the ad and inform the homicide unit if he was contacted by the caller again.

Based on this evidence, and the fact that "Hines" was on the note from Martin's house, Russell guessed that the H.J. Heinz Company could provide some information and contacted its records division. After a complete search of the company records, H.J. Heinz said it did not have anyone by the name of Cuffington or Hutzler.

That same day, Russell interviewed one of Martin's neighbors, a 30-year-old taxi driver named Kenneth Brooks. He reported that a woman who lived across the street from Martin told him she saw a taxi cab with a male passenger stop in front of Martin's home on the evening of November 12, 1973. The passenger was seen entering the home but was never seen leaving. Mr. Brooks could not provide any other information concerning the taxi cab passenger or the woman who reported that she observed this activity.

While all of this was unfolding, Russell received an anonymous call. The caller said he knew for a fact that Martin had placed an ad for a room for rent in *The Baltimore Sun* on November 11, 1973. Russell confirmed this information through the newspaper's business office. The small ad had been placed in the classified section and described a room for rent in the Hampden area with Martin's telephone number. The ad stated that an "employed refined gent" who did not smoke or drink was preferred.

Russell and Perkowski spent two weeks attempting to locate an informant or police official who knew of a suspect with the same mode of operation (M.O.) of committing crimes after the victim placed an ad for furnished rooms for rent in a local newspaper. A big break came in the case when Russell received information from another confidential informant that the name of a possible suspect was James Francis Smith, a white male in his fifties.

The informant claimed that Smith was responsible for Martin's murder. He based his belief on the fact that Smith had been arrested in Annapolis, Maryland, for a crime that had several similarities to this offense: An elderly female victim had been tied up, assaulted, and robbed in her Annapolis home several years before by a man inquiring about renting a room from her.

Smith had been arrested and convicted of this particular crime and was presently incarcerated in the Maryland Penitentiary for 12 years. The informant stated that Smith had an extensive record in various states, including an arrest for a homicide in Pittsburgh, Pennsylvania, in the early 1960s that was strikingly similar in many ways.

The informant further relayed that, although Smith was presently incarcerated, he was, in fact, on a work release program and would have had the opportunity to commit the offense. (A work release program meant that an individual inmate was released during the day or evening for purposes of employment at local business establishments and had the obligation to return to his institution at night.) The informant further provided the name of Smith's girlfriend as Carole Buffington. The detectives took immediate notice of the similarity in the name of Smith's girlfriend, Buffington, as compared to the name of Cuffington, which was on the note found at the crime scene.

To determine the details of Smith's prior conviction, Russell went to Annapolis Police Headquarters and interviewed Detective J. Craig, the principal investigator in the case against James Francis Smith (who was also known as James Lane). Smith had been arrested and convicted for the armed robbery of Mrs. Aspasia Nicholas and had been sentenced to 12 years for that crime. That file was retrieved and copies of all the documented facts and reports concerning the Annapolis crime were provided to Russell.

From the file, Russell discerned that Smith was a white male born on April 22, 1922, and was 51 years old at the time. He was five feet, nine inches in height, weighed 145 pounds and was of fair complexion.

At the time of his arrest in Annapolis, Smith had in his possession a newspaper clipping from a daily local newspaper that advertised Nicholas' room for rent. James F. Smith had listed two names on his prison visitor authorization card: Carole Buffington, his girlfriend who resided in Lutherville, Maryland, at the time and Helen Smith, his mother, who lived in Pennsylvania.

Craig provided Russell with several items of evidence that had been introduced against Smith in a previous Annapolis robbery: a black wallet with handwritten notes, a dress belt used to tie up the victim in the robbery, a signature sheet containing Smith's signature, and a letter addressed to Mrs. Aspasia Nicholas. Russell also learned that the informant had been correct: Smith had recently been approved for the work release program of the Jessup Correctional Camp Center.

On December 3, 1973, Russell further investigated Smith's status in the work release program by contacting the program's director, Mr. Sebastian Valenti, at Jessup Correctional Camp Center. Valenti verified that Smith had been approved for the work release program on November 6–9 and November 12, 1973. However, on November 13, Valenti had removed Smith from the program for violating the rules. It turned out that Smith was leaving the institution as though he were going to his job and returning as though he were coming from his job; however, Smith was not actually reporting to work. Smith had been removed from the program and placed back in "lockup" as a disciplinary measure. A few days later, he was moved out of the Camp Center and back to the Maryland House of Correction, since the Camp Center housed work release inmates.

The personnel of the Camp Center were not cooperative, and they refused to permit Russell to review Smith's institutional record without a Subpoena Duces Tecum (subpoena for production of evidence) under the signature of a judge. Although the homicide detectives thought this rather odd, they thought it was possible that it was merely an adherence to form, so they soon obtained the necessary legal order.

[Form image: Division of Correction Work Release Plan]

NAME	James Smith
NUMBER	113-073
OFFENSE	Armed Robbery
SENTENCE	12 YRS
DATE SENTENCED	9-25-69
EFFECTIVE DATE OF SENTENCE	9-25-69
COURT	Anne Arundel County Cir.
JUDGE	Evans
NAME OF EMPLOYER	Emerson's Restaurant
ADDRESS	Charles Center
TELEPHONE	727-0517
BASIC WORKING SCHEDULE	Mon-Sat 4PM-12 Midnight
BEGINNING DATE ON JOB	1-6-73
INITIAL HOURLY WAGES	2.50/hr
Initial job duties	Cook
Transportation provided by	State

The reckless work release plan for Smith, which enabled him to commit murder while still incarcerated.

On December 4, 1973, Russell went to the Jessup Correctional Camp Center and served Valenti with the Subpoena Duces Tecum. Copies of all Smith's institutional records were now his.

The records contained critical information. Through the work release program, Smith had been employed at the Emerson

Restaurant in Baltimore, and the job had been secured through the restaurant manager, Gary Shook.

Inmates participating in work release programs were required to sign in and out of the institution every day. The detectives obtained a copy of the log sheet, which showed that Smith did, indeed, sign out and back in every day from November 6 through November 13, with the exception of the weekend (November 9 and 10). On Monday, November 12, Smith signed out at 12:30 p.m. and signed back in again at 2:45 a.m. on November 13. Smith then signed out again at 2:30 p.m. that same day. However, after he signed the log book, he was detained by an institutional official and prohibited from leaving.

Valenti advised Russell that disciplinary action against Smith had been prompted because it had come to his attention that Smith had not been working at the Emerson Restaurant on November 7, 8, 9 and 12. Thus, Smith was in violation of the work release program rules, and he was unaccounted for by the work release personnel. Valenti also shared Smith's explanation for his unaccounted time with Russell. Smith said he spent the first day, November 6, working at the restaurant, but the manager told him the position had been disapproved since it wasn't full-time, and he was to return to the prison immediately. Smith said he spent the other days in question seeking new employment. His explanation could not be substantiated by the work release personnel or the prison, and, thus, was not accepted as credible.

On December 4, Kearney and Russell went to Jimmy's Cab Company on Chesapeake Avenue in Towson, Maryland, to follow up on the lead they got from Kenneth Brooks. They spoke to Paul Paciarelli, the dispatcher, and asked him about a driver's activities on November 12. Paciarelli informed the detectives that a cab driver named Richard Locke remembered taking a male passenger from the Towson area to the corner of Chestnut Avenue and Power Street in Hampden.

The following day, Kearney went to Martin's neighborhood to interview a neighbor, Katherine Hackley, who told him that she had had a telephone conversation with Martin around 4 p.m. on November 12. During that conversation, Martin told Hackley that she had rented a room in her house to a man named Cuffington. Hackley also said that Martin told her the man had called her from Hagerstown, Maryland, which is about an hour and a half west of Baltimore City. The man stated that his trunk would be coming from Pittsburgh, Pennsylvania, where he was employed by the H.J. Heinz Company and had just been transferred to Baltimore City.

The detective was beginning to sense a successful prosecution of Martin's murderer, James Smith. Hackley also informed the detective that she saw a Jimmy's Taxi Cab parked on Power Street and Chestnut Avenue between 5 and 5:30 p.m., and she thought a passenger was discharged. However, Hackley was not in a position to observe who, if anyone, got out of the cab. Hackley called Martin again around 9:25 p.m., but she failed to get an answer.

Locke, the taxi cab driver, had told Detectives Russell and Kearney that he could remember a male passenger on Monday evening on a date that he believed to be November 12. Locke recalled taking him to Powers and Chestnut Avenue. The passenger was a white male with a receding hairline, wearing some type of top coat and whose age he thought to be between 40 and 45.

Unfortunately, Locke could not remember exactly where he picked up this male passenger, but he was certain of the time and location because he regularly delivered a female passenger to that intersection. At that point in the interview, the detectives displayed a group of photographs they had brought with them. One of the six photographs was of Smith. The cab driver carefully viewed all six photos and selected the one of Smith. Locke initialed and dated the photograph on the reverse side, and all six photographs were placed in an evidence envelope. The detectives were invigorated by their efforts.

A few days later, Russell and Perkowski went to 3105 East Fleet Street.

Central records of the police department showed that there had been a robbery of a woman where a room for rent had been advertised at that address. On December 9, the detectives interviewed Mrs. Johanna Laegal, the victim of an assault and robbery on November 7. They showed Laegal the photographs they had previously shown Locke and asked her to identify her assailant. Laegal looked through all six photos and, without hesitation, picked the one of Smith, positively identifying him as her assailant. Laegal initialed and dated the back of Smith's photo.

But, the detectives were in no hurry to arrest Smith. At this point, he was in solitary confinement at the Maryland Penitentiary, serving his 12-year term for the 1969 armed robbery in Annapolis. They pursued their investigation diligently knowing they could arrest and charge Smith with the brutal murder of Martin at any time. On December 11, Russell and Perkowski went to the Emerson Restaurant and interviewed the manager, Gary Shook. Shook verified that Smith had been hired as a cook and worked one shift, on November 6, from 4 p.m. to 12 a.m. Additionally, Shook verified that Smith did not work on November 7, 8, 9, or 12, at any time during the day or evening.

That evening, the detectives traveled to Hagerstown to interview Carole Buffington, Smith's girlfriend. They went to her home, which was located in a rural part of Hagerstown and within actual sight of the Maryland House of Correction, where Smith was locked up. When the detectives arrived, Buffington was working, but they were greeted by Buffington's three teenage children, who let them in. When Buffington arrived 20 minutes later, she did not want to be questioned in front of her children, so the detectives accompanied her to the Maryland State Police Barracks for the interview.

Buffington was not what the police were expecting. She was a charming, polite, and attractive 41-year-old woman with a nice way of carrying herself. She was dressed very professionally, had an impressive job as the executive assistant for the Washington County Executive, and was obviously quite intelligent. At the State Police Barracks, the detectives questioned Buffington about her relationship with Smith and she gave a four-page affidavit. Although they were to deny it later, the detectives told Buffington that Smith was a psychotic, that he was very dangerous—and that he had brutally murdered Martin. They warned her to have nothing more to do with him and informed her that she had been very lucky that Smith had not harmed her.

This was the first time that Buffington had had any involvement with the police, and she was naturally deeply upset by what they said, even though she knew a fair amount about Smith's past life. Buffington told the detectives that she had some personal items belonging to Smith because the Camp Center had forwarded two boxes of his belongings when he had been removed from the work release program and forced to leave the institution. The detectives accompanied Buffington back to her house, where she located the two boxes from her basement. A cursory inspection revealed a blue-gray suit jacket that had apparent blood stains on it. The detectives inventoried the contents, gave Buffington a receipt and an inventory sheet of the items, and took the boxes with them.

It was an upbeat ride for the two detectives returning to Baltimore. For an hour and a half, they gloated over this newly found and possibly critical evidence, hoping that the blood stains on Smith's jacket would match Martin's blood type. Among the other personal effects they found were some newspaper clippings and personal papers belong to Smith.

In order to forestall any future legal disputes, the prosecutor and police prepared exhaustive applications for the search warrant and court orders they would need.

In order to obtain an order to extract Smith's blood, the detectives were legally required to file an affidavit explaining why they needed the sample. Apparently, to impress the judge, they filed a 14-page document, including many details of the case. Perkowski brought this affidavit and petition for the order to Judge Charles D. Harris of the local Supreme Bench of Baltimore City. After reading the affidavit and hearing from Perkowski and Gersh, the judge signed the order without hesitation.

On December 12, the detectives received a report that the blood on Smith's jacket was human blood Type A, which matched Martin. Nevertheless, they decided not to seek an arrest warrant charging Smith with Martin's murder just yet. Instead, they went before a local district court judge and secured an arrest warrant, charging him, instead, with the armed robbery of Johanna Laegal.

It was time for the detectives to confront Smith. At approximately 5:30 p.m. on December 18, the detectives arrived at the penitentiary to give Smith the statement of charges on the Laegel robbery charge and transported him to the homicide squad for the purpose of investigation.

There was some dispute as to what actually occurred at the homicide squad office; however, during the interrogation, Perkowski told Smith that he wanted a sample of his blood to determine his blood type. Smith signed a written statement to the effect that the blood on the jacket was his, that he was Type O, and they were welcome to take a sample of his blood to establish his blood type.

Smith guessed and hoped that he could bluff the detectives and, of course, further hoped that the blood on his jacket would match his own. The signed statement given to the police indicated that he had bumped his nose on a locker at the prison some several weeks before, resulting in the blood on the front right corner of his jacket. He also indicated that he had sneezed immediately after that injury, which accounted for the splatter pattern on his jacket.

That same evening, Perkowski and Russell, along with Assistant State's Attorney Howard Gersh, took Smith to Mercy Hospital, where a staff nurse removed two vials of Smith's blood, which did, in fact, prove to be Type O.

Upon Smith's return to the homicide squad after his trip to Mercy, he was finally informed that he was to be taken to the Eastern District Station to be charged with the murder of Doris Martin.

Smith and the officers arrived at the Eastern District Station around 1 a.m., and a sleepy-eyed commissioner heard the detectives briefly summarize their case and read what they had filed for charging Smith. When Smith was finally returned to his cell at the penitentiary, it was 3 a.m. Since he had no cellmate, he sat on his bunk and reviewed the charging documents in shock.

When he last sat on that bunk, he had every expectation of being paroled soon.

Smith remained in a rather stunned mental state for the next several days. Unlike the instances when criminal charges were placed against him in the past, he was indigent this time—financially unable to employ private counsel. He knew that meant he would be represented by an attorney from the Office of the Public Defender.

Christmas was a dismal day for Smith because Buffington, contrary to her prior practice of writing daily, had not written to him since December 15. When the detectives visited her, she stated that she no longer wanted anything to do with Smith. His only contact with the outside world had ended. He told cellmates that he was alone, and he was comfortable with that. However, he had written to Buffington, imploring her to come see him so he could explain to her that he was innocent of the charges against him. He thought of the "crim dick" phenomenon—the concept that some women become emotionally close to bandits and killers even though their good sense tells them to stay away—and hoped she would be swayed.

The next day, December 26, an investigator from the Office of the Public Defender interviewed Smith to establish whether he met the financial standards to make him eligible for the service of the Office of the Public Defender. Smith filled out the application form, but unknown to the investigator, Smith's instincts for survival were still working.

He knew of the public defender for the state, a criminal attorney by the name of Alan H. Murrell, who had been a prosecutor for several years in the 40s and early 50s. Smith was aware that Murrell had become the most prominent criminal attorney in the state of Maryland. Murrell was feared, not only because of his broad intellect and commanding presence, but also for his irascibility. He intimidated many local judges and most of the police witnesses who were subject to his harsh cross-examinations.

When the public defender system for the state of Maryland was initiated, Murrell took the opportunity to be head of that organization. Once he assumed the position of chief of this office, he spent most of his time administering the large staff across the state and suggesting reforms to the legislature. Therefore, he wasn't able to try many cases himself.

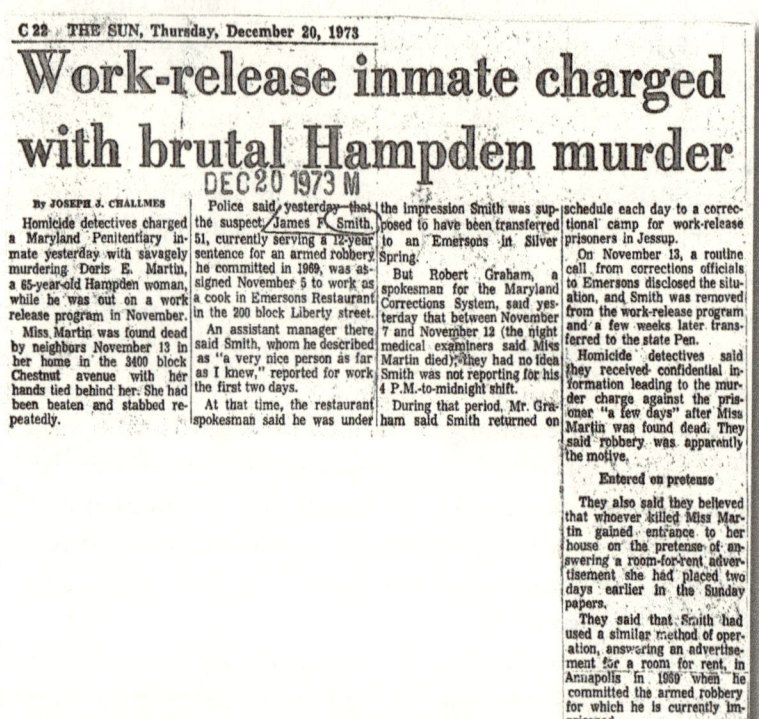

Article from the December 20, 1973, edition of *The Sun* outlining the crime and the accused.

Smith had decided that, if he was going to be represented by the Office of the Public Defender, he wanted to be represented by "the man himself." Smith was a prolific letter writer, and he wrote Murrell what would be the first of many letters regarding this case. It was a long and complimentary epistle, stating that he was "100% innocent" and asking Murrell to handle this case or personally appoint someone who would "believe him." Smith followed up with another letter in quick succession, once again, expressing confusion as to how he could be "tried on such a trumped up thing."

Room for Rent

In January of 1974, upon returning from a Florida vacation, I found a note on my desk from Murrell that he wanted to see me. Little did I know the amount of energy that I would expend as a result of those few handwritten words.

Chapter 2: Keating Defends Smith

When I saw Murrell on January 28, he gave me the letter Smith had sent him and requested that I investigate the case and defend Smith. Murrell said that, in his years around the courthouse, he had heard of Smith and his "con-man ways" and described him as a "bum."

At that point, Smith had not yet been indicted. His preliminary hearing at the district had been waived by the state, and his case was to be presented to the grand jury on February 5, 1974. I wrote to Smith advising him that he would be indicted shortly and that, prior to my interviewing him in person, I would learn all I could about the charges and evidence the state had against him. Our investigators supplied me with the original offense reports on the murder of Doris Martin and on the robbery of Johanna Laegal. I assumed that he would be indicted on both charges.

However, the witnesses in the Laegel case failed to identify Smith in a lineup, and, on February 5, the state indicted him for the murder of Doris Martin alone. That day, I filed my appearance formally in the case and knew once I did that, there was no turning back. Whatever happened, Smith and I were now a team, like it or not. Once counsel enters their appearance, it is difficult to withdraw it. By that point in my career, I had defended only 5 murder cases, but I had prosecuted over 50, and I was under no illusions as to what this case was going to entail.

The wording of the indictment was precise, and I knew I would eventually hear those powerful words read to twelve people selected as a jury. I could imagine the echo of the clerk's voice, and I understood that I would feel apprehensive when the clerk read the words aloud.

Smith also had been charged with, not only the first count—which charged first-degree murder,[2] second-degree murder, and manslaughter—but also with assault with intent to murder Doris Martin. The assault charge contained an administrative error, however. Smith was also charged with use of a gun during the commission of a crime of violence. I joked that I was certain I could win that count, since no gun had been used.

My investigation of the circumstances of this case could now begin in earnest, and I immediately filed several routine motions with some of the details we knew about the murder. Unfortunately, in 1973, the criminal discovery rules in the state of Maryland were woefully inadequate. Upon the filing of a discovery motion by defense counsel, the state was obliged only to give the names of any witnesses that it intended to call in the trial against the accused and not what they would say. They did, however, have to supply the substance of any statement made by the defendant. The state was also required to permit defense counsel to review any of the exhibits that were seized from the defendant and were intended to be introduced at trial. At the time, that was the extent of the defendant's discovery rights. In a dramatic demonstration of the perversion of written American values, a civil case, which doesn't involve the liberty or life of an individual, has more expansive discovery procedures. In a civil case, complete discovery of the opposing side's case can easily be obtained prior to trial.

The Office of the Public Defender had about 25 investigators who, upon direction or request of the staff attorney, performed

---

2. Normally, first-degree murder would carry the death penalty in Maryland, but Smith's good fortune with the criminal justice system prevailed again. In 1972, the Supreme Court, in Furman v. Georgia, declared that all death penalty statutes in each of the states were unconstitutional. It took several years before the "death penalty states" could pass legislation that would meet the new standards that would allow the death penalty. Doris Martin was murdered in 1973, during this short period before any such statute could be passed in Maryland, thereby making it impossible for the state to seek to execute Smith.

actual investigation for the attorneys. Many of these investigators were ex-police officers, ex-jail guards or ex-security men who performed their work diligently. When I was informed by the Prosecutor's Office in late January that Smith was to be indicted, I set preliminary inquiries in motion.

Our investigators located copies of the offense reports, revealing what the police had filed in both the murder and the unrelated robbery cases. These skeleton reports indicated only what the respective officers had found at the scene, but they did contain the names of the witnesses who would later be called before the jury.

Thus, on January 31, 1974, I sent our investigation unit 20 specific requests for information that I wanted in order to be adequately prepared to defend Smith. The local newspapers were searched for articles in reference to the killing. There had been extensive newspaper coverage of the case, not only because of its brutal nature, but also because the alleged killer, Smith, was on a work release program, and his actions reflected very poorly, to say the least, on the program. This, as it turned out, was likely the reason Valenti was so insistent upon receiving a Subpoena Duces Tecum before handing over Smith's files to the police.

Consequently, when the Jessup Correctional Camp Center was contacted by us to produce Smith's institutional records, it again refused to release records without a court order, but we obtained a court order and eventually acquired the records. We also obtained a copy of the newspaper advertisement that Martin had placed in *The Baltimore Sun*, interviewed the medical examiner to establish the exact time of death, and located and interviewed Johanna Laegal, the alleged victim of the robbery on November 7, 1973.

Officer Slawinski's supplemental report included the names and partial statements from three individuals. Of these three, I subsequently called two as defense witnesses. The first was a young man, 18 years of age, named Anthony Bateman, who told officers that he lived near Martin and that he saw a white male enter the victim's home around 4 p.m. on November 12. Our investigators had learned in early February that Bateman had entered the U.S.

Army and had been sent to California, and our attempt to locate him failed.

Slawinski's report also contained the name of Mrs. Mann, who was apparently a friend of the victim. The report noted that Mann had received a telephone call from the victim sometime prior to her death, but, unfortunately did not include the witness's full statement. Witness statements that are normally taken down at headquarters are not available to defense counsel. The individuals managing the work release program and the supervisor of Smith on that program were interviewed. Needless to say, they were hardly cooperative, again, likely due to the embarrassment of indirectly allowing the murder to occur despite their supervision.

The third individual, Esther Johnson, appeared in Slawinski's report. She was contacted because Slawinski noted that she had given a statement to the police in which she stated that she saw Martin walking her dog at 4:30 p.m. on November 12.

Since I was concerned about the defendant's easily proven scheme of using advertisements and then committing robberies after initial phone calls, I attempted to locate the record of telephone calls made by Smith at the Maryland Correctional Institute. However, we learned that the inmates used pay phones and such calls were not traceable to any individual.

That same day, I filed a battery of motions on behalf of Smith: Motion for Discovery and Inspection, Motion to Suppress Evidence, Motion to Suppress Any In-Court Identification of the Defendant, and Motion for a Speedy Trial. I also wrote to Smith telling him that I would meet with him to discuss the case once I received more information.

I soon received a very startling reply from Smith. His handwriting was very neat, a precise cursive with no errors in spite of an incensed tone. He was very articulate; it was very different from the normal correspondence I was accustomed to receiving from inmates. He stated that he was at a complete loss to know what was going on, and he could not understand how he could be charged with robbery and homicide since he "couldn't have killed that woman." His letter was full of paranoia, talking about the false charges that had been placed against him and that he was "damn mad about all of this."

He informed me that he had been taken before a lineup on January 16, and both witnesses had failed to identify him as the man they had seen. Subsequent investigation revealed this to be true. Locke, the taxi cab driver, and Laegal had been taken by Russell to view Smith in a lineup. I then located the photographs of the participants in the lineup. Since a public defender had been present, I also conferred with him. Although Laegal and Locke had both picked Smith from the photos, they failed to identify him in person.

Over the next couple of weeks, I busied myself with other cases and awaited the return of the information I needed to thoroughly discuss the case with Smith. Several lawyers from the Office of the Public Defender had been assigned legal interns, law students in their second or third year who were assigned to our office for clinical experience. My luck had held out as usual. Assigned to me for over a year was Kathy Koshell, a brilliant third-year law student. As we prepared cases together, I felt that I had a distinct advantage when operating in a male environment, since most males could not overlook her startling looks. She was very defense-oriented and wanted desperately to believe that each of our clients was innocent. I had some trepidation about taking her into a penitentiary full of several hundred hardened convicts who would go wild at the sight of any woman, but I decided to take her to meet Smith anyway. As we walked outside the main gate of the penitentiary, which was located in downtown Baltimore, Maryland, we could see the rows of cells just inside the long building. We could hear catcalls coming from many of the open windows, yet we could not discern any faces or people.

Upon showing identification, we were allowed to enter, even though the guards seemed to share my reservations about admitting my assistant to the penitentiary to see Smith, who was in the south wing, the administrative unit where he was in segregation for his own protection.

The penitentiary is a maximum-security institution housing the most dangerous criminal offenders in the state. Normally, when an inmate is in the main population, one can visit him in the attorney's and family's visiting room which, apart from the no smoking regulation, is quite comfortable. However, the rights of those inmates on segregation, whether for their own protection or for punishment, in comparison to other inmates, are greatly curtailed. They cannot work and many leave their cells for only a half-hour a day for exercise. They are allowed to shower only twice a week, are not permitted to perform any useful functions, and no recreation is provided. Theirs is a numbing and pathetic existence.

To visit inmates on segregation, it is necessary to be admitted into the main part of the institution with the typical cacophony of gates shutting and opening that comes with any journey through a prison. We were directed to a dingy visitor's booth, which was located just off the south wing. The room was about 30 feet long, and the attorneys are separated from the inmates by a thick, scratched, dirty piece of glass. Both the inmates and the attorneys were locked in and could not leave without the assistance of a guard. Eight telephones were located in the room; all were enabled so the speakers would hear each other.

Smith was waiting at the telephone when we arrived. He looked to be about 50 years old and was dressed in a working man's drab green. His fingers were heavily stained from nicotine and, as I expected from his photos, he was gray and slightly balding. He had the look and skin tone of an old-time con man, someone who has not received enough sunlight or a balanced diet. His teeth were disgusting and not taken care of, yet he had piercing blue eyes that conveyed vibrancy.

After listening to him for a few minutes, my intern refused to look him in the eye, which was very much unlike her. She was a little startled, as was I, when he discussed the rape charges with a shocking intensity. Later, I was to learn that he was an incessant talker with a verbal IQ of 129. Smith assured us of his innocence and told us directly that he was a con man only—that he had led his life by conning people, but that a con man would never kill anyone. He said he "could never see [him]self stabbing such an old woman to death," as he raised his clenched fist to the glass and made disturbing stabbing motions.

After he repeated that he was innocent in several different ways, several different times, I finally asked the guard to unlock the door, so we could return to my office. Koshell was beside herself. She got a really bad vibe from Smith, and, if I'm completely honest, I did too. Soon, she would ask to be removed from the case, and she would be spared what was to come.

In my line of work, you meet a lot of murderers. It sounds callous, but that becomes a non-issue in your evaluation of them. I could always look past their status as a killer and find something likeable, something redeemable in each one of my clients. But not this time. I could find nothing relatable in Smith. If I were pressed to say something positive about him, the best I could come up with would be his vibrant blue eyes. I decided to call him Jimmie in an attempt to humanize him. It was a trick I often use with a jury, but this time I was trying it on myself.

After leaving the prison, Koshell and I decided to contact the prosecutors to see what valuable information we could obtain in Smith's case. Since I had been a prosecutor in the State's Attorney's Office, I could generally have a reasonable discussion with them. They recognized that I understood it was their duty to prosecute vigorously. I knew that my approach had to be a subtle one. Though the evidence was overwhelming, and I was likely powerless to successfully defend Smith, I still had to be as prepared as I possibly could be to offer him the best defense possible.

Koshell and I walked through the Violent Crimes Liaison Unit where four experienced prosecutors were assigned. It was the duty of these liaison prosecutors to attempt to help the police wherever they needed legal help or advice, and it was these prosecutors who were always involved in the investigative phase of serious crimes. It was their function to gather enough evidence, so a trial prosecutor would not have to do preparatory work but could reserve his energies for presenting evidence. We arrived at the State's Attorney's Office on the third floor of the courthouse and located Assistant State's Attorney Howard Gersh, who had been in on the interview with Smith and Detectives Perkowski and Russell. Gersh was in his early forties and had extensive experience on both sides of the trial table. After the normal commotion which usually accompanied Koshell when she strode through an all-male office, Gersh took us into his office. The confident look and manner he used when he discussed the case contributed to my mounting concern that Smith was in a lot of trouble.

Gersh told me the case had been assigned to Sandy O'Connor, an attractive, young, redheaded prosecutor who was deputy head of the trial division. During our conversation, Gersh revealed a lot. He said he would not be personally involved with the trial, but that he would discuss it with me. Then, he began to gloat over the evidence and the work that the Prosecutor's Office and the police had done.

Arrogant, he could not resist arguing the state's case, informing us that they had an airtight circumstantial case against Smith. As he shared several previously unknown pieces of evidence that the state had, Koshell and I exchanged worried looks. Gersh told us about the statement Smith gave that the blood on his suit was his own Type O and boasted that they would prove the blood was, in fact, blood Type A, the same as Martin's. Gersh also informed us that, although Smith had denied any knowledge of the offense during the interrogation, he had also stated that he was sorry he had killed the woman, but that he would deny ever saying it if the police testified that he had admitted it.

Gersh then told us that, among the papers seized at Buffington's house, there was a piece of a newspaper containing classified ads. Several ads on one page had been underlined with a red marker and one of those underlined ads was Martin's. Gersh also noted that a red marker had been found among Smith's personal effects. Gersh kept going. He told us he would prove that Smith lived in Lutherville in 1968, across from the Heinz Company Factory, and that he had been born and had lived in Pittsburgh, Pennsylvania.

He mentioned the fact that Smith was not going to be charged with the robbery of Laegal on November 7 due to the victim's inability to pick him out of the lineup even though she had described him perfectly. Coincidently, Gersh said, Laegal had placed an ad in *The Baltimore Sun* for a furnished room for rent immediately before she was robbed.

Gersh was fully familiar with the defendant's 1969 conviction for armed robbery and indicated that the state would attempt to prove its case by the use of Smith's past con scheme or similar M.O. Further, he told us that Smith had a record going back to 1941, and he had been charged with a murder in Pittsburgh, Pennsylvania in 1962.

That crime involved a con game that used newspaper advertisements. The charge had been dismissed because Smith was incarcerated at the Alleghany County prison in Pennsylvania at the time the crime was committed. Later, though, Gersh learned, that Smith had been on work release at the time of the murder and, in fact, did have the opportunity to commit the offense. In addition, Gersh told us, he was prepared to prove that Smith had confessed to Buffington that he had killed a woman in Pittsburgh, Pennsylvania.

Gersh further told us that a woman who worked at the Keg of Ale, a restaurant near downtown Baltimore, was prepared to testify that she saw the defendant on November 12, 1973, at 8:30 p.m. The witness stated that she could identify him and had spoken to him, and that he had told her that he was from Pittsburgh.

Now, I *knew* Smith was in deep trouble.

Although I didn't know all the details of what Smith had told the police, they apparently had checked out his alibi for his whereabouts during the days he was supposed to be on the work release program and had interviewed all the people he had mentioned. Gersh informed us that many people did not remember Smith at all; others' recollections of the time that he was with them differed from the version that Smith gave to the police. Rather than continue attempting to take notes on what the prosecutor was telling me, I asked his permission to return to review the file, which the prosecutors would use at trial. Gersh agreed and said he would have it available for my review the following week.

I was annoyed at Gersh's gleeful, bragging manner, letting me know that Smith had no chance whatsoever.

On Monday morning of the next week, Koshell and I returned to the State's Attorney's Office and inquired whether Gersh was in. He was not, and we were consequently allowed by the secretary to take the file into Gersh's office and review it thoroughly. We made as many notes as we could in the hour or so we had before he returned. It was not Gersh's intention to show us the entire file, only selected parts of his choosing. Upon his return, we reminded him of his prior statement that we might review the file. We knew that we had been offered a golden opportunity, and we took it. Under the formal rules of discovery, we had no right to review the prosecutor's file, but at least now we knew the extent of the evidence facing us.

On March 8, I detailed all of the new information that I had received and wrote a letter to Smith asking for his explanation for the suspicious circumstantial facts. In my prior interview with Smith, he begged me to contact Buffington to ask her to contact him, distraught that she had decided to have nothing more to do with him. I had called her and had a brief conversation relaying Smith's request that she visit him just once, so he could explain why he was not guilty and how his lack of guilt could be proven. Buffington informed me that she was going to be called before the grand jury. Rather than get any substance of her material testimony, I decided simply to woo her and save that discussion for a future conversation. I wanted to impress upon her that I did not know what had happened, and I felt sympathy for her in that I had known of her close relationship with Smith.

Several days later, I received a response to my letter from Smith. In his trademark meticulous cursive, he indicated, once again, that he was innocent.

His letter greatly disturbed me, and I re-read it several times.

One example of the many precise and calculated letters from Smith to Keating.

Saturday Eve
March 16, 1974

Dear Mr. Keating,

I received your letter and after reading it was left mixed emotions. First and most important is that I am totally innocent of that crime regardless of the evidence the state claims to have. It is now obvious to me that the police will do anything to get a guilty verdict. Obviously because of the treacherous lie of saying, "I confessed to the crime but would deny it if they told." Can you in your wildest dreams picture (not only me, but any man) being questioned by detectives on a homicide charge, saying something like that and being able to leave without giving a signed confession? No way! From the very start of their questioning me about that woman's death, I vehemently protested and wanted an attorney because I was innocent. Det. Perkowski knows that. Even at the lineup (ask the Public Defender that was present) I was protesting because it looked rigged to me. I told Det. Perkowski even then, the worst crime is to convict an innocent man. He answered with a smirk, "If it's found that you're innocent I'll say, "I'm sorry" then laughed.

Also that lying cab driver you mentioned. The police must have something on him, for him to lie like that. Actually I hope he *don't* change his mind, and that he does say that I was in his cab about 5 pm on the 12th of November. Because I will *prove* beyond any doubt that he is committing perjury and will want him charged with that serious offense. I have an astounding letter from Carole Buffington that you *must* see. She was *threatened* by the *State* to testify.

So far I am disappointed, as I have heard nothing that has been done for me. I asked to have a few things checked by the investigators since Dec, but as yet they *seem* to be still checking.

As to Perkins State Hospital, I must see you in person before I say any more. I would also like a copy of all those news stories about me.

Again, Please no one thing, regardless of evidence on me, I *am* innocent of that crime. Can't get over that alleged note of Cuffington-Pittsburgh and Heinz. That is really and truly a lulu. I wonder who thought of that masterpiece of mystery. You said, (according to the police) the woman wrote it in her handwriting. I wonder? I read in the paper that she had a dog

name Buffy! Is that short for Buffington. Sure some strange things in this case.
Hope to see you soon.
James Francis Smith

P.S. My transcript of 1969, Carole had unless the police took it. Her number is 555-9199
Hagerstown after 7 pm[3]

The vehemence with which he protested his innocence was strange to me. I heard protestations of innocence in many cases; however, his continual, impassioned insistence did cause me momentary concern. What if he *were* innocent, and I failed to prove that he had not killed Martin? When you're a criminal defense attorney, innocence is always a possibility—no matter how remote. But, I *knew* this was a fantasy in this case, and I quickly dismissed that train of thought, never to return to it. Smith's reference in his letter to Clifton T. Perkins Hospital was in response to a suggestion that I had written that it would be worth his while to undergo a psychological evaluation since that could stall the trial and, perhaps, offer us a new avenue of defense (insanity).

And, it was important that we stall the case. I had heard that O'Connor was going to run for the state's attorney position in Baltimore County, and I much preferred to defend a case against a male prosecutor because you could strike harder blows during the trial without potentially alienating the jury. So, I decided to attempt to delay the case until she had resigned in Baltimore City. Stalling the case would not be easy, though, since I had already filed a speedy trial motion, as I routinely did on behalf of every client I represented.

---

3. Smith sent scores of letters written in his methodical and precise cursive to everyone involved in this case. Many of his letters have been included in this book, and they have been reproduced exactly in here, including the occasional spelling, grammatical, or punctuation error found in the original. The phone number has been changed.

Maryland law required that an individual who was serving time on another charge had to be tried on any new charge within 120 days of asking for a jury trial. Early in February, I had filed such a motion on Smith's behalf and had sent the requisite certified letters to the chief judge and to the state's attorney. Since a court was required to dismiss a case if this 120-day period was not observed, the state was very careful about complying with such motions in order to protect their case from such a dismissal. Once the time had started to run, it could only be stopped for "good cause."

The case was promptly set for a trial that was scheduled to start on April 22, 1974. Soon, I learned that my client, against his own best interest, was acting independently. Without seeking my advice or even informing me, he wrote to the chief judge of the Supreme Bench of Baltimore City on March 24. The letter detailed my advice that we stall the trial, stated I had not done any work on his behalf, and advised the court that he did not want me as his attorney. He stated in his letter:

> *Now your Honor, it is not like my trial is over and I am voicing dissatisfaction with my attorney. I am voicing it now and there is certainly good reason for it. Going on over four months and I have seen him once. Does that sound like interest in my case? I am not interested in how busy he is with other things; there is a homicide charge against me and that's what I'm interested in. If he has no more concern than what I have been shown, then he should let someone else handle it. Certainly if I had five to ten thousand dollars, some lawyer would be interested. Now I realize that the defender's office will be angry because of this and I won't be sure of getting the help I need, therefore, I want to express my constitutional right of self-representation and to act as co-counsel with the lawyer who represents me. As to this day I have never received a copy of an indictment and as yet have been not been to Court to enter a not guilty plea.*

Unfortunately, this letter was not forwarded to me for some time. When I finally did receive it, I wished that I'd had it when I went to see Smith for the second time on April 1. If I had known its contents and had the letter with me at that time, I would have been able to put him on the defensive and make future control of him and, therefore, the case easier.

Not knowing about the letter, I explained the advantage of going to Perkins Hospital to Smith. I thought that if he had brutally stabbed Martin, he might, in fact, be criminally insane. He listened carefully as I discussed the pros and cons of going to the hospital for a 60-day evaluation. I advised him that it meant he would have to waive his right to a speedy trial and that there might be some difficulty in later court proceedings if he admitted the offense to the psychiatrist. After a brief conversation, he indicated that it was probably the best course of action to take. Even then, however, he did not ever mention the letter he had already sent to the chief judge.

As I left the penitentiary that day, I felt relieved. Since Smith's trial would not be rescheduled for several months, that time would allow my investigators to accumulate all the information I would need to effectively defend Smith. I went directly to the Prosecutor's Office and talked to O'Connor, explaining that the defendant should be brought to court as soon as possible because he had agreed to change his plea to not guilty by reason of insanity.

Smith's arraignment was scheduled for April 11, 1974.

Chapter 3: Smith's Criminal History

Before Smith's arraignment, I received disturbing information. The Oklahoma State Police were looking at Smith in connection with the murder of an elderly woman that had occurred in November 1973. Soon after, I was advised that the Oklahoma Police had determined that Smith did not commit that crime. I also learned that a homicide squad in New York was considering Smith a suspect in another murder.

I learned from the Heinz Company, independent of the police investigation, that no one by the name of "Buffington" or anything close to it had ever been employed by that company and that there was no company in the entire state of Pennsylvania with the spelling "Hines." I also received information concerning Smith's past criminal conduct.

The Office of the Public Defender in Annapolis, Maryland, delivered its entire file on Smith's 1969 armed robbery case to me. It included the police reports and the evidence that the police had presented at Smith's trial, as well as copies of Smith's appeal and the post-conviction action he brought against his attorney in that case, charging that the attorney had been incompetent and had failed to render effective assistance. I knew from those allegations that, if Smith were to be convicted of murdering Martin, I could expect that he would then turn on me. By writing the chief judge and complaining about me before trial, he was subtly preparing for an attack upon my professional competence, just in case.

I received, from the state, an answer to the discovery motion I had filed on Smith's behalf. It provided the names of 70 people who might be called as state's witnesses. Upon receiving the list, I placed each name on a separate piece of paper and then attempted, as is my standard preparation for a trial jury, to describe everything I thought these witnesses would say.

One of the primary witnesses was Carole Buffington. I had had three conversations with her on the phone. She informed me that she had received several letters from Smith and that one of them concerned his defense. In the letter, Smith told Buffington that the reason he could not prove his innocence before was that he was scared that she would break off their relationship when she learned where he had been on the night of November 12, 1973. I later learned, from reading letters she had sent to Smith prior to November 13, 1973, that she had assumed he had another woman and had cheated on her. He explained in one of his letters that, on November 12, he committed a crime in Virginia, but that it was not a crime of violence. Rather, he had flimflammed some woman out of a couple hundred dollars, and he had gotten the woman's name from a newspaper ad in *The Washington Post*. Smith had written to Buffington thinking that she would know the reason he had to have the money he stole.

From my conversation with her, it was clear that he had borrowed several hundred dollars from her. He claimed to have given the money to a prison official named Andretti as a down payment for an early parole. Smith also informed Buffington that he had not wanted to admit to the crime in Virginia since no one knew he had committed it, and it would assuredly prevent him from getting an early parole. Buffington also told me that she had testified before the grand jury that Smith had admitted to her that he had killed a woman in Pittsburgh in 1962. When he attempted to con the woman in Pittsburgh, he became scared of her reaction and apparently strangled her to death. Buffington sent me his recent letters and past legal papers, so I could review them.

At our second interview, Smith had informed me about the crime in Virginia that he had committed, but the news about the prior murder was new—and it disturbed me greatly. I attempted to contact the District Attorney's Office in Pittsburgh to gain as much information as possible about that case; however, they said the Baltimore City Police Department had the file and to contact them. I knew, of course, that the Baltimore City Police Department would never let me review that file.

During my trial preparation, I sent a note to the investigators reporting that Smith was in Arlington, Virginia, pulling his con game at the time of the Martin murder. Smith had told me that he left the Trailways Bus Terminal at 4:30 p.m. on November 12, 1973, and that he had picked out the woman who was looking for a boarder in *The Washington Post*. He described her as a white female in her late 60s, who was overweight and had a red bag. He also told me that he had gone to this woman's house, where he managed to talk her into loaning him $300. During their initial phone call, the woman indicated to Smith that an FBI agent was also a tenant in the house.

In a letter to Buffington, which subsequently became an exhibit at trial, Smith suggested that he could have her do some detective work on his behalf. In it, he requested that "Brat," as he fondly called her, "locate a copy of *The Washington Post* and bring it to him." She informed me that she would send this important letter to me, as she felt I was in a better position to undertake such an investigation. When I received the letter, I asked the Chief of Investigation, Jim Watkins, to obtain a copy of *The Washington Post* for November 9, 10, 11, and 12.

Watkins, a young black man, short in stature, was recently elevated to the head of the Investigation Unit. He supervised approximately 20 individuals, but once he saw how excited and concerned I was about Smith's case, he devoted himself fully to it. He was very creative in the field of investigation and dropped by my office each evening to discuss whatever latest piece of information he had discovered. Not only did he provide me with written reports, but he was also a good sounding board for my ideas. Before my newspaper ad lead could be fully explored, the arraignment date arrived, and I found myself—for the first time—in court at Smith's side.

Chapter 4:
In Court—First Appearance

The day of the arraignment, April 11, arrived, and Smith's case was scheduled to go before Judge Paul Dorf. It happened that I was also scheduled to go before Judge Dorf later that same day for a different matter: the sentencing on a rape case I had lost some several weeks before. This case was one where I had grown to like the client, Mollar, and had developed a close relationship with him.

Mollar was charged with grabbing two women off the street, on two different days, and pulling them into alleys and raping them. I managed to persuade the state to dismiss one of the cases on the basis that the identification was too weak. Several weeks before this sentencing date, we had impaneled the jury in the case. The trial had gone on for two days, and I was sure the jury was going to acquit my client, but it turned out that someone on the jury knew the defendant's brother, and a mistrial was declared. The jurors assured me that they had just been waiting for the opportunity to acquit the defendant.

Unfortunately, when the case was re-tried, the jury convicted Mollar of the rape as the result of several of the judge's rulings in the case. He, in my mind, was clearly wrong on a point of law, and I immediately contemplated an appeal. With all that tension regarding the rape case hanging in the courtroom, I knew I was in for an uneasy afternoon.

Dorf came onto the bench at 2 p.m. precisely, and I asked to approach with the prosecutor. As we were standing there in conference, discussing the Mollar case at the bench before the open court, Smith was brought up from the "bullpen" (a modern-day slang term for a dungeon where 25 defendants are kept in the basement of the courthouse awaiting trial). Smith entered through a side door in handcuffs and leg irons. He made a pathetic picture, and I recognized by the way he looked angrily over at the bench conference that his arraignment would not pass without some incident.

By the time the bench conference concluded, I determined that the judge did intend, as I suspected, to give Mollar the maximum sentence of 21 years. My day was not going well, and I was, to say the least, feeling aggressive and testy. I returned to the trial table and said hello to Smith. Mark Kolman, the prosecutor, arose and stated that he was present in court to represent the state on behalf of Ms. O'Connor, who was engaged in another trial at that time, but that she intended to prosecute the case. (O'Connor did eventually resign from the State's Attorney's Office of Baltimore City to successfully campaign for the office of State's Attorney for Baltimore County and, thus, removed herself from any participation in Smith case.)

Kolman explained to the court that a plea of insanity was to be entered by the defendant. Since Smith's indictment charged him with murder, it was mandatory that the entire indictment be read formally to him in open court. The clerk asked Smith if he had received a copy of the indictment. Even though I had shown Smith the indictment and had explained all its elements to him, Smith responded, "I have not. Never seen one." I stood to explain to the court that I had, in my hand, a copy of Smith's indictment and that I intended to copy it and send it to him. The court then ordered the clerk to read the indictment.

No matter how many times I had heard the words, they always sounded formidable to me. While it is not required that an attorney stand up when a clerk is reading an indictment to a defendant, I always made it a practice to rise with the defendant as a symbolic gesture to the court, as well as a commitment to the defendant, that I was with him—from the placing of the charges in open court to the rendering of the jury's verdict and subsequent sentence. Smith and I rose.

The clerk read:

> *The jurors of the State of Maryland, for the body of the City of Baltimore, do on their oath present James Francis Smith, late of said City, on November 13th in the year of our Lord 1973 at the city aforesaid, feloniously, willfully, and of deliberately premeditated malice aforethought, did murder Doris Martin contrary to the form of the act of assembly and in such case made and provided and against the peace, government, and dignity of the state. In the second count, you are charged with assault with intent to murder. In the third count, you are charged with assault. In the fourth count, you are charged with violation of the handgun law.*

The clerk then inquired, "Counsel, the plea?"

Carefully phrasing my words, I stated, "The plea would be not guilty, if it please the court. I have prepared a plea of not guilty generally, not guilty by reason of insanity at the time, and not guilty by reason of the fact that the defendant cannot understand the nature of the proceedings against him."

I had prepared a written plea of insanity, had it in my hands, and was handing it to the clerk when Smith asked the court if he was allowed to speak. The court informed him that I had already entered his plea on his behalf, but Smith was clearly annoyed. "I'm not pleading! I'm not pleading to insanity!" Smith insisted.

I indicated to the court that I had visited Smith at the penitentiary a couple of weeks prior, and we had come to a mutual understanding as to the plea at that time. I told Dorf that Smith had just then relayed to me his change of mind, and it was clear that he was displeased with my proposed method of proceeding. I asked the court, nevertheless, to allow me to still enter the insanity plea on his behalf. Smith jumped to his feet and stated to the court:

Your honor, I was told several weeks ago that my trial was due the 22nd of this month. There's been no preparation in my case whatsoever. This is the first time I've been to court. I have never received an indictment, I am not guilty of the crime, and I am not pleading guilty. It would be insane for me to plead guilty for something I didn't do ... If I plead not guilty by reason of insanity, that's the same thing as saying I did it, that I wasn't sane. I am pleading not guilty, period*!*

At that point, Dorf asked Smith to take the stand and he was sworn in. I was momentarily stunned by Smith's comments. It was a total fabrication for him to say that he had not seen the indictment and that there had been no preparation in this case. In fact, I was well prepared, as I had been for every case that I've ever tried, as a prosecutor or defense counselor.

Lying came very easy to Smith and he was continuing his con game with the judge.

His protestations of innocence made it clear, once again, that if he were found guilty, he would just claim I had been incompetent in a post-conviction proceeding, and I would have to justify my own actions. Regardless, I aggressively represented him. I had to.

I had been criticized by clients in the past. A public defender does not normally command the same confidence and trust as a private lawyer. In fact, there is a feeling among defendants that public defenders do not provide aggressive representation and that they are in collusion with the state.

Smith could not have been more mistaken in my case. Although I knew the prosecutors and had worked with each of them, I have a combative and competitive spirit, so I fought them vigorously nonetheless. Winning is everything to me, no matter what I'm doing. Not to mention, it was my duty to represent all my clients to the best of my abilities, and I took that responsibility seriously.

I was angered to hear Smith try to embarrass me in front of the judge. I informed the court, after Smith's complaints, that I had filed 6 preliminary motions on his behalf and interviewed 40 of the state's witnesses. There was a lot more I could say. However, not wishing to place my client in a damaging position, I simply noted that I thought Smith's statement, "that nothing had been done in his case," was inaccurate.

The court, questioning Smith, attempted to explain the ramifications of pleading not guilty by reason of insanity. Dorf clarified that one does not admit the offense simply by entering such a plea. Further, the court explained that he could not be tried for the crime itself if he were to be found insane at the time of the alleged commission of the crime.

Smith, demonstrating his intelligence, cunning, and understanding of the law, in his general aggressive behavior stated, "I understand that, Your Honor. I understand I have been sent to an insane asylum and that would be it." Smith went on, "Well, sir, believe me, I am not guilty of this crime and I am sane, and I don't have to go to no institution to find that out."

After further repartee between Smith and the court, I could see the judge was annoyed. Having expected this to be a simple five-minute procedure, Dorf attempted to re-explain to Smith what a plea of not guilty by reason of insanity meant legally. Smith, getting more aggravated and excited by the moment said, "I'm not pleading not guilty by reason of insanity." The court attempted, once more, to get Smith to agree to the entry of that plea, but Smith was adamant. After that the court asked, "Do you understand me?" Smith stated: "Yes, but Your Honor, why is it, I mean in my case, that it seems they insist upon wanting me to go to Perkins?" He expressed that he didn't want to be examined; he just wanted to go to trial. He asked the court, "The idea is I'm here for arraignment; is that correct?" The court indicated that he was right.

I found it rather amusing that Smith was now questioning the judge, and I silently admired the way he was handling himself. I began to grow concerned, however, that the judge would be persuaded that the trial should go on as scheduled as Smith went on to say, "The way I understand it then, the judge sets a date for trial. I have been told my trial is coming up in 10 days. I have had no preparation or nothing. I don't think that's fair. I want to plead not guilty and I want to have time for the attorney or defender's office to prepare this case properly. That's all I am asking. I am definitely not going to plead insanity to something. Like I said, it would be insane to do something like that, as I have no knowledge of the crime. I am in my right senses, and I am not guilty of the crime."

Smith again repeated that he didn't want to be examined at all and merely asked the court to be fair with him. The court immediately recognized the complicated legal issue involved. Because Smith was incarcerated already, the Intrastate Detainer Act required that he be tried within 120 days or the case would be dismissed. The judge saw the legal difficulty in committing a man for evaluation against his wishes when he had such a limit of 120 days within which to try the case. It was my hope that this legal issue would become a central issue, but I said nothing for fear of displaying or limiting my legal hand.

The judge told Smith that he would have to waive his speedy trial rights under the detainer law if a plea of insanity was issued. The defendant, in a final attempt to clear up the matter for the record, stated, "Your Honor, you mean if I don't plead what you're saying, this insanity, I'll have to go to trial in 10 days on the 22nd?"

The judge told him that he was correct, and Smith responded that he was willing to waive his right to a speedy trial. Smith clearly repeated that, saying, "I'll waive that and give you more time, but I am not going to do it to plead guilty in order to give time by going to a mental hospital."

With these few words, he had completely eliminated the legal argument I had planned to pursue at a later hearing. I saw it necessary to immediately influence the court to preserve the issue despite Smith's misguided words. I cited a section of the Maryland law on insanity, which permits any officer of the court to suggest anything within his own knowledge that might assist the court to make just rulings in any particular case. I indicated to the court that I would not have filed such a plea if I did not think it was necessary to protect the rights of Smith. The judge, picking up on my cue, noted that it was obvious that I had certain strong feelings about this mental examination. Smith couldn't resist stating, "Yes that's what's worrying me."

The judge, by now, was red and visibly angry at the length of time and the hassle at what should have been a simple arraignment. "What's worrying *me*," he said, "[is] I happen to know this attorney. He is a very able and conscientious lawyer."

I felt relieved that I had prior experience with Dorf, and he was going to support me. Smith, however, went on to say, "If he does this, I don't want him. I told him I wrote to the chief judge … two weeks ago, explaining this to him. I am not guilty of the crime. I don't want it on the record that I am pleading guilty to insanity, whether the attorney likes it or not. I want to have faith in my attorney. If he doesn't act in my best interest—what I think it is—I would rather not have him and get someone else. This is a capital case.[4] I haven't seen him or an indictment. Today, I just heard the indictment read off. All this time, since November, I heard nothing. I heard something about a gun, a uniform gun law—I never had a gun in my life."

The judge interrupted Smith and stated, "Alright, what I am going to do is this—"

Smith interrupted, "I want to plead not guilty and have a reasonable amount of time to prepare this case, that's all I'm asking."

The judge, once again, carefully explained to him that if the trial did not go off as scheduled for any reason, he would have to waive his rights under the detainer law. I observed and listened carefully to the judge's words because I knew he was making a record for any future legal issue on this point. "The two of them can't be done. If I accept your plea of not guilty, I cannot give you a reasonable time to prepare the case unless you waive the detainer law."

"I will waive the detainer law," Smith said.

Dorf had picked up my cue and responded to my earlier comment about the officers of the court and indicated that he was going to allow me to plead as the defendant wished: not guilty.

---

4. As previously noted, the state could not seek the death penalty for Smith, so his was not actually a capital case. Smith was aware of this, and this statement was undoubtedly a calculated exaggeration on Smith's part.

The court also noted that, on its own volition, as a matter of the court record, it was going to refer the defendant to the Clifton T. Perkins Hospital for an examination strictly for the benefit of the court. Smith exploded, stating:

Your honor, I'm being—the state's attorney wanted this to begin with! Somebody is in cahoots to get me to Perkins! I'm not going to be examined by no psychiatrist at Perkins because I am not going to answer no questions. I come up here for a plea, which is my right to enter a plea. I'm pleading not guilty, period. I don't want to be railroaded to Perkins. I'm not saying nothing there. I don't care what they do to me. You can put me in a straitjacket or what. I'm telling you right now it's going to be the same thing. I'm not guilty. I want to go to trial, and I want to have a reasonable amount of time to prepare my case. If this attorney is going to sell me out with the state's attorney, I don't want to have anything to do with it. I'd like to get a proper attorney. I'm not guilty. The state, they figure if I go and get a state psychiatrist to say he's insane, they could lock the door on me. I'm not taking that chance because I'm not guilty and that's it! I'd rather face a jury.

The prosecutor, bristling like I was that our professional integrity had been attacked, informed the court, for the record, that the State "ha[d] not at any time requested that this man be sent any place." More comments were exchanged between the court and the defendant.

I noted that Dorf had become more conciliatory in tone, explaining that a plea of not guilty by reason of insanity could be dropped at a later time. However, when Smith attempted to interrupt the judge, he became short with Smith stating, "Now let me finish." After several minutes of this more moderate tone by the judge, Smith, in violent display of temper which disturbed me greatly, told the court:

Your Honor, I appreciate what you just said. I have reflected as you went along. I have reflected. I don't want to make the court angry, but I have already made up my mind. Actually, I know that after a trial is over a man can go up and say I object because I wasn't satisfied with my lawyer. I'm saying this now. I am definitely not satisfied with my attorney! I do not want to go to Perkins. I'm in my right state of mind. I had nothing to do with it, I'm not guilty. I'm not going to let a doctor examine me. I mean I'll stay mute if I'm sent there, so it will be a waste of time to send me. I'm ready. All I want is a trial date set within a reasonable time to give me a chance to prepare this case properly. I would like another thing—my constitutional rights. I wrote your Chief Judge Foster letting him know that I would like to act as co-counsel with my attorney because there's a lot in this case that hasn't been discussed with me. I have seen this attorney maybe an hour since December, since my case was sent to the Defender's Office. It's certainly isn't enough time to prepare the case. I'm asking in a nice way; I'm not pleading guilty, period. I would like an attorney really appointed, someone who has experience. This is a young man. I need someone like Mr. Rosenthal.

When I heard those words from Smith, I was flushed with anger. Instead of maintaining a cool courtroom attitude, I let my temper get the best of me. As a public defender, a free lawyer, I had learned to deal with abuse whether it took the form of verbal comments in court or written communications to judges. I was secure in my reputation with the court and the fact that I always represented each client as if I were representing myself. Given all the work I had done and my interest in the case, I felt I needed to defend myself. I jumped to my feet, threw down my folder, and said, "I would gladly give my file to Mr. Rosenthal. Rarely do I asked to be excused from a case. I don't intend to take this."[5]

A defense lawyer cannot take into account the possible vicious propensity of his clients, for if he is unduly concerned with that, his mind will be detracted from his advocacy. However, as far as I was concerned, not only was the defendant lying, he was engaging in courtroom combat. I glanced at Smith and saw a bewildered and angry look on his face. The judge, after establishing once more that Smith was willing to waive the detainer law and completely ignoring my outburst, told the witness to step down from the stand. Dorf then stated a summary of what had occurred and said he was prepared to sign an order committing Smith to Clifton T. Perkins hospital for a psychiatric examination. He added, "The court … will not allow Mr. Keating to withdraw his appearance because the court is familiar with Mr. Keating's background, his ability. The court feels he will give this man able and proper representation. The court will ask Mr. Keating to discuss anything with the individual."

Undaunted, Smith was again on his feet, gesturing with a finger and yelling, "I am not going to submit! I'm being railroaded before the case starts! This is all what the state's attorney wants! He (indicating me) corroborated with the state. As for my attorney, I am sorry, I would not like to have him!"

---

5. This would not be the last time Smith and I argued in front of Judge Dorf. In another colorful incident prior to jury selection, Smith started to indicate, once again, that he didn't want me to represent him. I had good credibility with the court from my years as a prosecutor and a defense attorney and Smith's actions were transparent. I knew how to resolve the issue. I had to be in control. In order to dominate Smith, I said, "That's quite alright. I will just burn your file and you can rot in prison." Smith told me I couldn't speak to him that way. "I just did, and you can go fuck yourself," I said. He was incensed. It's my property," he replied. "No, it's not; it's my work product. You come back tomorrow and tell me what you want to do."

The next day, as we came back in and reassembled, Smith pandered, "Look, man, I'm sorry. I'm sorry. You and I need to get together. I like you as a lawyer. You're a good lawyer. I'm really sorry about that." I told Smith to forget it and we could move on. He insisted on apologizing to the court. Again, I told him to forget it, but when the judge came down, Smith stood up and said, "I want to address the court." He proceeded to tell the judge, "I feel as though I've done Mr. Keating a wrong, and I didn't mean to be so critical of him." He continued to throw praise my way, again incurring Judge Dorf's impatience. I don't know what he thought the display was going to get him, but what it did was elucidate once again just what kind of a manipulative game player I had on my hands.

Again, the judge attempted to speak to Smith, but he interrupted stating, "I want a proper trial. If I had money, Your Honor, this wouldn't be going on right now. If I had the money—"

Dorf interrupted, "If you had the money and if you had a million dollars ... you couldn't hire a better lawyer. Let me tell you something Mr. Smith, and listen, listen closely to what I am telling you, all right? I don't intend to repeat it. Mr. Keating is going to be your attorney. If you don't want to talk to Mr. Keating, that's your right not to talk with him when he comes over to see you. Mr. Keating will then advise the court that you refused to discuss the case with him. Mr. Keating will sit alongside of you at the trial table, you understand me? If you want his representation, you'll have it available. If you don't want his representation, you can do as you see fit. But your case is going to be set in promptly. Now I would advise you to be very wise because it's your life that's involved and your liberty that's involved. I would advise you to think very strongly before you refuse able representation."

I felt validated by Dorf's comments for purposes of the record. Yet, Smith was undaunted. He looked at the judge with contempt and asked, "Are you the judge in the case, Your Honor? Are you going to be the judge?"

"I don't know."

"Well if you are, I would like it in the record I would like you to be excluded."

The judge indicated that his sentiment could be placed in the record, and Smith continued, "I want that noted in the record because I see you are already prejudice against me, forcing me to go to Perkins and forcing me to have somebody who only talked to me one hour since September. Is that proper representation?"

Dorf had finally had enough. He cut Smith short.

"Gentlemen, we are finished with this case."

Smith did not look at me as he was led away from the courtroom in handcuffs by two guards. I was angry at myself for not having remained calmer through the proceeding. But, in a very real sense, I admired Smith because he was attempting to take on professionals in their own milieu, and he showed no fear and no awe for the title of lawyer or judge. He was obviously intelligent and articulate, and I recognized that he could probably bear up under the tension of a long trial. His personal attacks on everyone led me to believe that the psychiatrists would find him insane and classify him as paranoid, giving me escape from attempting to argue away the voluminous circumstantial evidence the state had accumulated.

Smith disappeared behind the door to the bullpen, to be returned to the penitentiary. Different guards appeared with my rape defendant, ready for sentencing. Prior to the sentencing phase, it was necessary for me to argue a motion for a new trial on Mollar's behalf. Unfortunately, I did not achieve my goal. Dorf promptly denied my motion for a new trial.

It had been a long day. When I got back to the office, I reflected with my feet upon the desk. I knew that Smith's case would not be ordinary. I knew that it would continue to take a great deal of my energy, as it already had. I could expect the unexpected in an environment where the unexpected had grown commonplace. I was glad to have Smith's arraignment over.

Five days later, on April 16, I received a letter from Dorf that included a copy of a letter Smith had written to him on April 14. Dorf indicated that he had sent a copy of Smith's communication to the Prosecutor's Office as well and suggested that we all meet in order to head off any difficulty with Smith.

The letter from Dorf to the prosecutor said:

> *In view of the enclosed letter from Mr. Smith I would advise that you contact Mr. Keating immediately and set this case in for a speedy trial. It seems obvious that you will not get any cooperation from the defendant. It's doubtful whether he will consent to examination. I am specifically concerned about his statement, "I said I would waive a speedy trial right, providing I did not go to Perkins." Even though I believe this statement to be inaccurate, I see the handwriting on the wall and therefore am advising this case be set in immediately.*

In his letter Smith indicated that he said he would only waive his speedy trial right if I were removed from the case and insisted that he did not wish to go to Perkins and, therefore, his constitutional rights were being violated. He spent two pages criticizing the lack of preparation in his case. Upon receiving the letter, I walked over to confer with Dorf in person, and he gave me the best possible advice for the situation: to protect my own representation in Smith's case by detailing everything I had done on his behalf. I did not want to discuss the waiver issue with the judge, since I was not about to give up any viable legal issue on behalf of Smith. Instead, I indicated that I would arrange a meeting between myself, the judge, and the prosecutor at a mutually convenient time.

When I returned to my office, I immediately took the judge's advice and spent three full hours reviewing my file and documenting the dates and times that had been expended by the Office of the Public Defender on behalf of Smith. Although it angered me to waste valuable hours, I felt it might be necessary at some future date. By the time the post-conviction proceeding took place, I would have long forgotten all of the actions that I had taken on behalf of Smith.

I also took the time to detail to Watkins what had transpired and explained that Smith was going to Perkins for an evaluation, whether he liked it or not. Watkins informed me that he had copies of *The Washington Post*, November 9, Evening Edition, and he showed me a group of ads for furnished rooms for rent listed under both Alexandria and Arlington, Virginia. Since I questioned whether Smith would cooperate with me, I asked Watkins to personally go to Perkins to show Smith the paper and ask him to point out which group of phone numbers he had selected his victim from.

It also occurred to me that it might be a good idea to have Watkins as a witness in the case if I could find any excuse whatsoever to call him. Since the jurors in Baltimore City were predominantly black, I felt that it could not hurt to have a sharp, black man testify and thereby create the inference that he believed that Smith was innocent in a case where a white man was charged with murdering a white woman. It could only assist Smith if Watkins's presence merely offset any latent racial prejudice any of the black jurors might harbor. I had learned as a young lawyer that it was the ultimate conceit to attempt to navigate in a fantasy world, rather than the real one, when it came to race.

I had filed a Motion for Speedy Trial generally and had also supplied Smith with typewritten letters for him to sign for certification by the chief judge and state's attorney that he wished a speedy trial under the Intrastate Detainer Act. In reviewing Smith's file, I also learned that, in February, Smith had filed his own Motion to Dismiss pursuant to the Intrastate Detainer Act. He had failed to inform me of this, and it became clear, once again, that he was attempting to be his own lawyer. Reviewing the typewritten form Smith had created for his motion, I recognized just how intelligent and devious he was.

Meanwhile, I had asked our investigation department to find all the locations of a Heinz Pickle Co. in the country. I wanted to remove the connection of a Heinz Pickle Co. being located in Pittsburgh, where Smith was born and raised, and the Maryland branch being located in Lutherville, across from his girlfriend's house. Unfortunately, our investigation department discovered that there were Heinz Company manufacturers in Cleveland and St. Louis, but that Heinz Pickle Co. was located only in Pittsburgh, Pennsylvania.

My gamble had not paid off. I was certain that I was sure to hear more about Heinz Pickles before Mr. Smith's story had concluded. It was to be, however, a long time before all the details and factual investigation that I required could be performed. I hoped Smith would cooperate with the officials at the state hospital and that they would find him insane, thereby avoiding the necessity of a protracted trial. But our investigations continued since we knew that Smith had stated that he was not going to cooperate with the psychiatrists.

Much to my regret, I did not contact Perkins to see if Smith had been comfortably housed there, preferring, rather, to have a minimum amount of personal contact with Smith. On June 9, 1974, Dorf's bailiff sent me a copy of another lengthy letter from

Mr. Smith, written in his painstakingly perfect cursive. It read as follows:

> *Dear Judge;*
>
> *I would appreciate if you would go to your records of April 11, 1974 (or you might recall). In any event I want to try and refresh your memory. I was charged with the crime of <u>Homicide</u> on <u>December 19, 1973</u>. The next day I wrote to the Public Defender's Office for help concerning this charge that I am completely innocent of. An investigator came over the next day and said an attorney would be assigned to me. When weeks passed without seeing an Attorney I wrote several letters but to no avail. Not until February 21, 1974 (two months later) did attorney Anton Keating show up saying he was to represent me. He spent less than one hour with me, telling me he would visit the State's Attorney's Office to see what they had.*
>
> *He said he would file a few motions, speedy trial, suppress evidence and a couple of other motions. I had no time to tell my whole side as he was in a hurry. A couple weeks more passed without seeing Mr. Keating. I again wrote letters, but not until April 1, 1974 did I see him. He told me there was some woman Prosecutor that he didn't want to go up against, and said she was due by July to be transferred to Federal Court, and that his advice (since <u>he</u> also wanted more time—he had since February—actually their office (Public Defender) had since December, was for me to enter a plea of "Not Guilty by Reason of Insanity" and that I would be gone for a couple of months and then could change my plea. I told him for me to plead guilty "would in FACT BE INSANITY" because <u>I'm innocent</u>. He kept telling me it wouldn't hurt me, and the plea would be changed. I told him it would show on the record and my answer was NO that my plea would be "NOT GUILTY PERIOD." He said I'm your attorney and that's my advice think it over, and he left. None of the case was discussed except my asking him to check my whereabouts at the time of the alleged crime (which was supposed to be in*

confidence) and he would see I couldn't have done it. He said he would check and left.

Low and behold on <u>April 11, 1974</u>, I was brought before you for <u>arraignment</u>. I was under the impression that an arraignment proceeding consisted of reading the indictment (I still have not received a copy of that) then the Judge asking if I had a lawyer, then to ask what the plea was and whether a court or jury trial was wanted. After that to hear the date he sets for trial. Now that is what I have been led to believe an "arraignment proceeding" is.

When I entered your Court, Mr. Keating and a State's Atty were conferring with you at the bench. When I sat down at the table the discussion ended, and Mr. Keating came and sat beside me. You spoke up and asked the clerk to read the indictment. You asked if I had rec'd a copy. I said "no." Your clerk said there is no record of his receiving a copy. <u>Mr. Keating</u> stood up and said "<u>I have a copy and will run one off for him</u>." <u>(That has yet to be done.)</u> Then you asked what the plea was? Mr. Keating said "Not guilty by reason of insanity" and it's recommended that he be sent to the Perkins Hospital. I'm sure you can recall (because I was shocked) my jumping up and saying; Hold it! That's NOT my plea! My plea is <u>Not Guilty for the reason that I'm NOT</u>! Mr. Keating said; "I'm sorry Your Honor I thought—but you broke in and asked me to take the stand. (I recall it <u>All</u> vividly).

You then started telling me of my Constitutional Right to be evaluated at the hospital, and that it couldn't hurt me etc. I said: "Your Honor; my plea is not guilty. I want a fair trial like anyone else, and refuse the Perkins offer because I am sane and innocent." As your tape will recall, I resented your remark: "You mean you were sane at the time." I know nothing of the time or crime, but I know I'm sane was my answer.

Before I entered your court I was astounded to find that April 22nd was to be my trial date (only 11 more days, and no preparation of my case whatsoever after all those months, so that date was set before arraignment.

Now you said; will you waive your right to a speedy trial? I said yes on the condition that <u>Mr. Keating be removed from my case as he has sold me out</u>, and that I don't go to Perkins. I tried to have Attorney Rosenthal assigned to me. Mr. Keating jumped up, slammed the folder down, and said; let him have Rosenthal! And you said then you will waive your speedy trial right. I said yes, you shocked me when you said; "I will accept your plea of Not Guilty but order you to Perkins for evaluation and Mr. Keating will be your lawyer whether you want him or not. I know him and he is a good lawyer." I said Your Honor, it's a waste of time sending me to Perkins because I will remain Mute and talk to no one. I made you angry when I said; are you to be the trial judge in this case? You said you didn't know? I said well if you are, will you please remove yourself as I can see where you stand!

That night I wrote you a letter saying; I felt you overstepped your bounds in that proceeding, and that since my conditions were not met, I therefore did NOT waive my speedy trial right (as your tape will show).

On April 16, 1974, I rec'd an answer from your bailiff saying; "Judge Dorf has received your letter of April 11, 1974 and is looking into the matter for you." When I heard nothing further from you, I again wrote on April 22, 1974. I again received from your Bailiff the following:

JUDGE DORF IS IN RECEIPT OF YOUR LETTER APRIL 22, 1974, and WISHES TO ADVISE YOU THAT HE HAS CONTACTED THE STATES ATTY'S OFFICE IN REFERENCE TO YOUR MATTER. YOUR CASE WAS ORIGINALLY SET FOR APRIL 22, 1974 IN PART I, but WAS REMOVED BECAUSE OF THE CONTEMPLATED PLEA OF NOT GUILTY by reason of INSANITY. WE HAVE ADVISED THE STATE'S ATTORNEY to set this MATTER IN FOR TRIAL AT THE EARLIEST POSSIBLE DATE.

Judge Foster acknowledges my speedy trial by a letter dated February 22, 1974. After a month passed in your court and I was not transferred to Perkins, I assumed it was not going to be. It will be 2 months since that day on Tuesday. <u>In all that time since April 11, 1974 when you overruled me and said Mr. Keating would be my attorney, I have heard not one (1) single word from him</u>. Something is radically wrong, because I was informed that <u>tomorrow the 10th, I was to be transferred to Perkins</u>.

Had I went in April I would now be back. My rights certainly are being jeopardized. I have no preparation for my case, but the 120 days (speedy trial) is up on June 22, 1974. I hope something is done about this. <u>I don't know Habeas Corpus form. But I would like this to be considered as such and be given a hearing</u> with Mr. Keating present.

Respectfully,
James F. Smith, #113073.
P.S. By the time you get this I will be at Perkins.

I was naturally disturbed by the fact that Smith had not yet been transferred to Perkins for evaluation. I assumed the transfer had taken place and had marked on my calendar to check with the hospital after the two-month period necessary for evaluation to discover what the results were. I recognized the predicament I was in. Smith was waging an all-out battle to embarrass me and, if he were to be convicted, to accuse me of incompetency.

I immediately contacted Perkins and found out that, as Smith had stated in his postscript, he was then at Perkins undergoing evaluation. However, in order to stave off his post-conviction suit against me, I wrote him a six-page letter detailing everything that had been done on his behalf in the case. I started the letter after referring to Smith's letter to Dorf by stating, "Just so the record will be clear, this letter will serve to rebut many of the things you stated in your letter to Judge Dorf." I then proceeded to detail every single thing the Office of the Public Defender had done on Smith's behalf, including all telephone calls, conversations, meetings, statements, witnesses, and other items of evidence. I concluded the letter by stating:

> *I totally disagree with your version of the manner in which I interviewed you at the Maryland Penitentiary ... On both of those occasions, I discussed the State's case against you.*
>
> *I have been assigned to represent you by the Public Defender for the State of Maryland and I take that responsibility very seriously. As far as I am concerned, you are innocent of the charges pending against you until the State proves you are guilty beyond a reasonable doubt and to a moral certainty. I would strongly suggest that instead of attempting to build a case against me for Post-Conviction purposes, that you cooperate with me in the defense of your case.*

We were engaged in a game of cat and mouse of sorts. It was my hope that Smith was intelligent enough to see that this letter could be used as evidence in a subsequent post-conviction case and that—just by the sheer volume of work that had been expended on his behalf—Smith would have no opportunity to say that his attorney was unprepared. I rushed my letter to him after it had been typed and, almost immediately, I received a response from him. My mail on Thursday, June 20, 1974, included the following letter written to me by Mr. Smith:

> *Dear Sir,*
>
> *I just received your letter dated 6/18/74. This is the first word I have had since 4/11/74. I went over the letter as thoroughly as possible. There have been <u>many</u> contacts made, (according to the letter) by both the police and your office that I don't understand, and there are many names that have been mentioned that are new to me.*
>
> *I would like you to know I "<u>fully</u>" resent your last paragraph stating; "I strongly suggest that instead of attempting to build a case against me for post-conviction purposes that you cooperate with me in the defense of your case." <u>That</u> was definitely uncalled for, since a post-conviction proceeding had been the furthest thing from my mind, since I am Totally Innocent of the charges that are against me. I am NOT a MURDERER, as a matter of fact, I am not even capable of*

such an offense! Since the shock I rec'd on December 19, 1973, (when I was informed of the charge,) a case in (some mysterious way) has been building up against me. Strand by Strand I have been entwined by a web. In a small way, I have been responsible for a couple of those strands (since I did not know at the start of the talk by the detectives on the Eve of Dec 18, 1973, (I was building up to the present case), therefore I lied when I was asked about my whereabouts on November 12, 1973. I surely (then) wasn't going to tell them I was in Alexandria Va. breaking the law when no one knew anything about it, (And that is where I was on the 12th). first to Wash D.C. then to Va. Anyhow, if someone could bring a recorder and let me go back to the time of work release until the present, they will see that something is radically wrong. I am almost convinced some prison official (or Officials) have been feeding the police with information to get me out of the way. I am sure (now that I have heard of the Tipton case) where the wife paid (alleged) $15,000 for a parole for her husband, but got only work release. Similar to that; "was ME" which was on record BEFORE the above mentioned case came to light.

I too have paid $$, the first payment of just $200.00 was made last Sept. or Oct., another $800.00 was paid on NOV 12th (somewhere between 10:30 p.m. and 11 p.m.). Then all <u>hell</u> broke loose the next morning (13th) when Mr. Stritch, my class. officer had me transferred to the Maryland House of Correction. Oddly, I saw His name mentioned (newspaper) in the above case, along with Mr. McColley, Deputy Commissioner.

Anyhow, if someone would take the time to hear my FULL COMPLETE story (and also Mrs. Buffington's—she has written and sent me $ and stamps since I last saw you, swearing she loves me and always will). My story would show that there is more to this than meets the eye. Someone wants me out of the way, and an opportunity came up when that poor woman was murdered. You must remember that *according to the news media and the police, she was murdered on either the 12th or 13th or whenever. I was checked in on the 13th and I heard nothing until December 18th about the case, and then was charged on the 19th of December. Since then it has been a nightmare. I did NOT murder anyone and do not seem to be able to get anyone to listen. I do <u>know</u> the police have LIED as to my giving a statement and saying I verbally confessed. I VEHEMENTLY protested the charge over and over saying I knew Nothing about it. And I did NOT (knowingly) waive any rights by signing a form that was read to me. I was asked if I understood what was read and then signed that I understood. After <u>that</u>, Mr. Perkowski wrote in yes or no after each question. (That was <u>before</u> I was questioned.) When he brought up Murder, I then asked for an Atty. He said, Look it says no after the line read, "Do you want an attorney present?" I said, "I wasn't asked if I wanted one, I was asked if I understood what the line said. Nevertheless, Something is Totally Wrong. I am Completely INNOCENT of the Charge.*

I have been trying to get out of Perkins. I don't belong here and the Doctors know it. My right to a speedy trial was NOT waived since Judge Dorf did not grant my request of NOT being sent here. I would like 2 things. To give a complete story on tape, and to be able to call the 4 Alexandria, Va numbers that are in the paper of Nov. 9th. (This should have been done months ago).

I am <u>not</u> trying (as you stated) to build a post-conviction case, since I have NO thoughts of being convicted of something I don't know about.

One more thing, I have "CITATIONS" that will show that Mr. Perkowski had NO RIGHT (even if Mrs. Buffington gave HER permission) to seize my personal things, without my consent. And they knew where I was!

I have tried unsuccessfully several times to get my reading glasses and bifocals from Mr. Perkowski, I need them badly.

I am hoping that something is being done about the case as it has gone too long.

Sincerely,
James F. Smith

P.S. I just (finally) talked to an investigator from the Public Defender's Office.
I have refused to sign papers here or to talk to a Psychiatrist or Psychologist. I tell them I want to be returned to the Pen. I also told them my plea is NOT—" Not Guilty By Reason of Insanity" that my plea is—Not Guilty because I'm innocent period.

With each letter from Smith, I became more and more concerned. He was documenting everything involved with the case, which meant I could not lapse in my meticulous documentation of everything as well. I immediately attempted to obtain Smith's glasses for him from the homicide squad office, but they would not release his personal property seized in Hagerstown since they envisioned a potential legal problem based on their giving up some pieces of evidence and not others. I could understand the rationale behind their decision, and I was forced to accept it—at least until we got into a courtroom.

The next day, Watkins told me he had interviewed Smith and discussed his alibi, which was that he was in Virginia, committing larceny, at the time of the murder. There were four or five telephone numbers under the Furnished Room for Rent section in *The Washington Post*, November 9, 1973, Evening Edition. Smith told Watkins he couldn't recall which number he had called, but it was one of those four or five.

Watkins then relayed a startling fact. When he returned to the office, he had selected the first telephone number and called it. The woman who answered, a Mrs. Virginia Sullivan, was not very cooperative and, after a two- or three-minute conversation, Watkins decided she was not the right person. When he had asked her if she had ever rented a room to a man from Baltimore, she indicated she hadn't. Near the end of the conversation, however, she revealed that—right about the time in question—she had been robbed by a man who had come to rent her room.

We immediately attempted to obtain a current photograph of Smith. We had the option of sending our investigator over to Perkins to take a photograph; however, I decided against that course of action. Instead, we contacted the Homicide Squad, but they refused to give us a current photograph and instead supplied one from when he was booked for the armed robbery in 1969. That photo was five years out of date and did not fairly depict Smith. I felt that even if Sullivan could not identify the photograph of Smith, I would be able to make a circumstantial case that he had, in fact, been the individual who had robbed her. I could then accuse the police and the State's Attorney's Office of being unfair by not providing a current photograph and, thereby, reduce the impact of her failure to identify him. I knew there would be some difficulty getting Sullivan to cooperate because she had indicated that she did not want to be bothered anymore and did not wish to appear in court, since she was rather old and suffered with arthritis.

Pursuant to Smith's request, I sent an investigator out to visit him with dictating equipment. Smith was then allowed to dictate his side of the story to his heart's content. When the tape was returned, I listened to it carefully.

Meanwhile, the investigator drove to Alexandria, Virginia, to discuss the alleged larceny with Sullivan. Her recollection of the manner by which money had been taken from her differed to a large extent from the version Smith had given. While it was true that she lived close to the Masonic Temple (as he had indicated that his victim did) and that she had received a telephone call from a man who wished to rent her room, the details of what happened when the man arrived were in dispute. Photographs of Smith were shown to Sullivan, and she indicated that he was not the man who had taken her money.

We knew that Smith's typical modus operandi was to pose as a man being transferred by his company in order to con money out of unsuspecting, older women who rent out rooms. Sullivan indicated that the man who had come to see her sometime around the end of November fit this pattern and eventually took a couple hundred dollars that she had on the kitchen table and ran out of the house. Unfortunately, Sullivan first stated that she thought the incident had taken place 10 days before Christmas. It was noted by the investigator that—if it had been 10 days before *Thanksgiving*—the date would have been November 12. Sullivan was obviously confused as to when the incident happened. Since she had not reported it to the police to avoid the inconvenience of court and police procedures, she had no frame of reference with which to pinpoint the time of the crime perpetrated against her. Additionally, the time that she gave (about 5 p.m.) did not coincide with the time Smith had given us and did not, therefore, provide him with a complete alibi. I was also greatly disappointed that she was sure the photo of Smith was not the man who had robbed her. I knew that I had to contemplate very carefully before proceeding. Watkins made several more calls to Sullivan, and she began to grow adamant that she could not come to Baltimore and that she did not want to be involved in the case.

The prosecutorial team was grinding away in its preparation for the trial. O'Connor had indeed left the office and an assistant, Mark Kolman, who had been the attorney in court during Smith's arraignment already, was assigned. I believed that, while Kolman was a sound prosecutor, I would have the advantage all the way through the trial. My only prior case with him had been an armed robbery charge where the defendant had refused to come out of lockup to be tried. That defendant, Larry Roberts, had been brought into the courtroom in manacles since it had been necessary for five guards to drag him to court, and they hadn't been able to do so without the use of mace. He was as shocked as I when the jury acquitted Roberts.

Needless to say, the trial of Larry Roberts left an indelible impression upon both Kolman and me. I had no doubt that he would not take this case lightly and that, in fact, he would work very hard to beat me.

Kolman had two individuals assisting him: Gary Jordan, a law school student assigned to the Prosecutor's Office, and another student who took a lesser role. I was soon to learn that Jordan, while he could not actively participate in the trial of the case since he was still a student, was an exceptionally bright man who had graduated from Dartmouth as an undergraduate.

As the trial date approached, I received, from the Prosecutor's Office, an amended answer to my discovery motion on June 28, 1974. No longer did the state have 70 witnesses, but they gave me the names of 5 more individuals in this supplemental answer to my discovery motion. I noticed, with some interest, the names on this amended sheet. They included Patricia Opdyke, Susan Ostradovec, Margaret Neal, and Marie Mayo. I was curious to know how they fit into the scheme of the trial and immediately assigned my investigators to interview these women. What we learned was very disconcerting. Jordan, on his own initiative, had reviewed some of the state's evidence and the newspaper clipping that had been found in Smith's pockets when his property had been seized. Jordan assumed that, since Smith had allegedly called Martin, he might have also called other women whose names were underlined from that same newspaper. He thus set about contacting these individuals to see if they had, in fact, been called by an individual who wished to rent a room. It seemed that his investigation and inspiration paid off for the state.

Our investigation revealed that Susan Ostradovec lived in Pasadena, Maryland, a township not far from Baltimore. She told our investigation department that she was recently contacted by the State's Attorney's Office in Baltimore City, who indicated that her name had been found in evidence taken from the suspect in a homicide. Ostradovec stated that she had been contacted by a man who used the name "Buffington" sometime in November 1973 in reference to an advertisement she had placed in *The Sun* newspaper. She stated that the man said he represented a firm whose name she could not recall. Ostradovec made an appointment for the man to view the room, but the appointment had not been kept.

Marie Mayo also indicated that she had been recently contacted by the State's Attorney's Office regarding a newspaper advertisement she had placed in *The Sun* papers for some rental properties she managed. She remembered that a man called on a Monday or Sunday evening and said he would call back. While she couldn't remember the exact time of these calls, she did recall that the man said he was from the Heinz Company and had six employees coming to the area. Mayo stated that the man never showed up. Patricia Opdyke informed our investigators—with some venom—that a subject who identified himself as a Mr. Murray called her on November 2, 1973, in answer to an ad she placed in the Baltimore newspapers for rooms for rent. "Murray" told her that he was the foreman of an Alaskan pipeline company and stated that his employer, James Dunn, a surveyor for the Alaskan pipeline company, would be arriving in town with other employees. The caller indicated that he wished to rent all available rooms for a period of two years and that a check in the amount of $1,800 had been mailed to her address for Mr. Dunn. Opdyke revealed that "Mr. Dunn" arrived at her house on Calvert Street in Baltimore City at approximately 4:30 p.m. that day. She was alone except for an elderly owner of the property who was in a chair in the kitchen. Dunn looked around and agreed to take all of the available rooms. He then became very flattering and affectionate to Opdyke, and she admitted that she fell for it. Dunn then stated that he needed money to get his surveying equipment before it was returned to Annapolis. Opdyke said she did not keep much money in the house, but she did give him $65. My investigators also found out that Gary Jordan had called her in reference to the ad. She told him she had never reported the flimflam to the police, and the prosecutor sent Russell to display photographs for her to identify "Mr. Dunn." She immediately picked Smith as the thief and gave her rental book over to the officer.

Margaret Neal, also contacted by the Prosecutor's Office, could not recall the substance of any conversation she had in reference to the renting of her room. For that, I was extremely grateful.

After gathering all of this information, I wondered more and more how I was going to extricate Smith from his predicament. It seemed the longer the state had to prepare its case, the more evidence it was digging up against my client. I knew the trial date was rapidly approaching and, consequently, set about assigning legal research assignments to the people who were available to me in the Office of the Public Defender.

Carl Maio, one of our lawyers, had told me in the past that he was not satisfied working in the Appeal Section of our office and that he wished to work on a homicide case with me. He was about 27 years of age and very bright—and had the best credentials I had ever seen. He was a member of several bars, including bars in Italy, France, and the Netherlands. Additionally, he was a member of the bar in Massachusetts, Pennsylvania, and Maryland, although he had only been admitted to practice in Maryland the year before. These facts alone were unparalleled in my experience, and I recognized that he could be of great assistance to me. I asked him to research several areas of the law, so we would have memoranda prepared for the trial of the case.

On July 1, I received a copy of the report that Clifton T. Perkins State Hospital had filed in the case. Dr. Robert H. Sauer, M.D., Superintendent of Clifton T. Perkins State Hospital, authored the report. He indicated that Smith had been admitted to the hospital on June 10, and that Smith had received a fairly complete psychiatric evaluation despite the fact that he had refused to cooperate with psychological testing and a social service investigation. Sauer indicated that Smith had been presented to a Medical Staff Conference on June 28, 1974, and it was the unanimous opinion of the medical staff that he was able to understand the nature and object of the proceedings against him and to assist in his defense. It was also the unanimous opinion of the medical staff that he did not suffer from a mental disorder at the time of the alleged offense of such severity to cause him to lack substantial capacity to appreciate the criminality of his conduct or to conform his conduct to the requirements of law. The official diagnosis was no mental disorder and that Smith was not suffering from a psychosis or severe neurosis. Based on that report, I could not even raise an insanity defense on behalf of Smith, even if he had elected to allow me to do so.

I decided to interview Sauer and traveled to Perkins myself. During the course of our meeting, I learned that, instead of the normal 60 days which it takes to evaluate a potentially "crazy" person, Smith had been observed for just 17 days, and he had not cooperated with the psychiatrists or the psychological testing at all. Sauer indicated that a social worker had discussed background information with Smith for about a half hour prior to his admission, and Sauer had personally seen him for an hour the day he arrived. Apart from that, no other person had interviewed Smith since he stated he was not going to cooperate.

Based upon those one-and-a-half-hours of interviews with no outside investigation, it was concluded that Smith was sane and could stand trial.

After talking to Sauer for approximately an hour, I was then led into the visitor's room and Jimmie appeared before me. I stayed with him for hours, going over the evidence against him and the results of our various investigations. He seemed resigned to the fact that I was going to represent him, and I began to feel that, perhaps, he and I would not fight during the trial after all, thereby giving him more opportunity to escape life imprisonment.

Chapter 5:
Smith Psychological Profile, Family & Personal History

The Department of Correctional Services for the state of Maryland's Reception-Diagnostic and Classification Center is located at the Maryland Penitentiary. When an inmate is being sentenced, he arrives at the center for evaluation and an admission summary is written. While reading one of these summaries for Smith, I gleaned a wealth of information about his background.

Born in Pennsylvania on April 22, 1922, Smith was first of four children born to the union of Michael Smith and Helen (Gavigan) Smith. His father worked as a crane operator in a steel mill and, although Smith did not know the extent of his father's education, Smith contended that his father was literate.

Smith's three sisters, Ursuleen, June, and Rita, were all at least six years younger than him. He was reared by his parents until the age of 14, when his father was killed in an automobile accident.

The family resided in a working class residential section of the industrial town of Braddock, Pennsylvania, which adjoined Pittsburgh. He contended that the delinquency rate in his neighborhood was very high, but he got along well with neighbors and playmates, played in the nearby streets and parks, and was a Boy Scout for three or four years. According to Smith, his leisure time was taken up with reading and playing chess.

Finances were short during the Depression and, after his father's death, only necessities were provided. His mother was a dominated marital partner and a strict disciplinarian who said Smith was fairly obedient at home, although he acted more uncontrolled in the community. After his father's death, Smith's mother lived in a common-law union with a mill worker, and Smith admitted some difficulty in accepting his stepfather, inspiring him to leave the home, although they related better in later years. Smith admitted to a fair relationship with his sisters and said he was told that he was the mother's favorite, although he never felt he was treated that way.

Smith obtained his elementary schooling in St. Brundus, Pennsylvania. He denied having any failures or being suspended, but said he was truant frequently. He claimed that he was mostly a B student but admitted that his conduct was poor. Verification from St. Brundus School stated that he completed the seventh grade, but that he repeated grades one, four, and seven and rated poorly scholastically. According to them, he did receive a D rating in conduct. The principal, Sister Ursulena, also remembered that he had stolen money now and then and said that his mother had a hard time with him at home. Smith also claimed to have completed the tenth grade and entered the eleventh grade at St. Thomas School in Braddock, Pennsylvania. Shortly thereafter, Smith left Pennsylvania and ran away with a magazine crew. He reported that it was that experience that gave him the idea of stealing from people by approaching them in their homes.

According to the files, Smith claimed to have been inducted into the U.S. Army in 1944, serving in the infantry until 1945. He denied any disciplinary reaction and claimed he was honorably discharged. Smith credited himself with a rating of corporal and quoted his serial number as 33893304 (this remains unverified).

Upon leaving the Army in October 1945, Smith married his first wife, Lois McBride Smith. Smith related that they had money problems and were eventually divorced. They lived together for two years and had two children, James and Thomas, born in 1946 and 1947 respectively.

Smith eventually deserted his wife when he absconded from parole, and she divorced Smith in 1950 on grounds of his incarceration. Smith claimed that he was married for the second time, in 1956 in St. Louis, Missouri, after a courtship of two months. The wife developed cancer of the womb six months after the marriage and began to drink excessively. There were no children from this marriage.

Smith claimed to have lived in Braddock with his parents—and, later, just his mother—until 1961, when he moved to Columbus, Ohio. He wasn't there long before he went to Baltimore in 1963. Indeed, when Smith was not incarcerated, he moved about considerably.

One of the later reports offered insight into Smith's employment history. Smith claimed he had jobs in the past but could not recall them very well. Anne Arundel General Hospital in Annapolis, Maryland, had employed him as an operating room orderly. While there, Smith liked to make himself seem more important than he was. He was called on the carpet for representing himself as an anesthesiologist, and he merely pawned it off as a joke and promised to correct the false impression. Nevertheless, the hospital rated him as a reliable employee whose work performance was excellent, and they stated he was overqualified for the job. They added that he had an unusual ability to quiet children down before surgery. They also relayed that he dressed extremely well and was able to communicate effectively, making an excellent personal presentation. Yet, they said they would not rehire him and recommended that he not be released in the Annapolis area because of the ill feeling toward him in the community.

Multiple reports offered a clear impression of Smith's personality. In one report, the examiner's conclusion was that Smith was an alert individual who had a better-than-average intelligence. During the interview, Smith was extremely frightened and worried, as he was in protective custody because he had testified against correctional officers at the Maryland House of Correction who were indicted on drug charges.

Numerous psychological reports were also contained in these official records. The last such report, dated February 13, 1974, was written by the chief psychologist, a certified psychologist for the state of Maryland. The report stated:

> *This inmate was first known to the writer in 1964 when a psychological custody was done on him and the report is dated June 12, 1964. At that time these intelligence tests were in the normal range, with the full-scale IQ of 113. However, the [verbal] score was 16 points higher than the performance score [129], indicating a very glib persuasive individual. All of the scores were high except the score in picture arrangement, indicating poor ability for social judgment. The low score of the object assembly test indicated that he is a cold, ruthless rejecting individual who is wholly egocentric and hedonistic. This man has no feelings whatsoever for the rights, privileges, and feelings for others. His only use for other people is to manipulate them to his own advantage. He only seeks power and prestige and his own emotional gratification. He is incapable of loving anyone in the genuine fashion.*

According to the report, a personality test verified the conclusions and indicated a very evasive, antisocial individual. It was stated that Smith was:

> *... a very aggressive individual, and with his glibness, he will undoubtedly work his way into a position of power and prestige among the inmates. This man is a liar and swindler of longstanding. He should not be allowed to obtain any assignment which would give him access to confidential information. He is a smooth persuader of other people to stir up trouble while he stands back and watches the action. This is a thoroughly anti-social hedonistic individual who is a real sociopath.*

Another study was conducted on Smith in October 1965. In conclusion, this study stated:

> *Smith has had a poor adjustment within the institution and has spent much time in segregation. The present psychological study with test administered on the 6th of September 1965, reveals the same result as stated in the initial psychological report. There are absolutely no indications of rehabilitation, and he must be classified as a habitual criminal and parole is not recommended.*

The report indicated that he showed a pattern of earning certain privileges in prison based on good behavior. But, as soon as the restrictions of maximum security were eased up and he achieved some degree of freedom, he would repeatedly violate the trust placed in him.

The Minnesota Multiphasic Personality Inventory (M.M.P.I.) Test is a widely used personality test in the mental health field. When administered to Smith, the results indicated that he was a sociopath with extremely high dependence upon women and alcohol. He was always searching for a way to "get rich quick." His history showed that he was a habitual gambler, and the results of the MMPI indicated that it was doubtful that he would ever cure himself of the gambling habit in a free society. The report stated that Smith was a very inadequate individual and there were "very strong signs that if he is allowed to be in a free society for a very long time he would be susceptible to drugs like amphetamine barbiturates and hallucinogens such as LSD."

The Bender Visual Motor Gestalt test was also performed. This test indicated that Smith was a very egocentric individual who liked to do things the way he wanted, without regard to any instructions or rules. His test indicated, like most psychopaths, that it was difficult if not impossible to change his habits once he formed a pattern of behavior.

The House-Tree-Person Test and the Draw-a-Person Test indicated a man with abnormal aggressive tendencies who had very strong feelings of hatred and hostility towards females. The report said:

He is very dependent upon the female but only because he feels that he can swindle money out of her more easily than he can out of males. There is an abnormal amount of sexual preoccupation in the personality and the strength that he shows in the drawing of the naked male, along with the other psychical aggression, indicating that he has a great many fantasies of rape which he would [act on] ... if the opportunity arose. In free society, he tends to have rather grandiose feelings about his attraction to women and he feels quite slighted or personally injured if a woman does not give sex to him freely.

The Rorschach Psychodiagnostic Test indicated that Smith had a very vivid, aggressive fantasy life while incarcerated. As soon as he was out of confinement, he stopped realizing sexual drive in fantasy and began to relive the fantasies in reality by acting out his sexual aggression. As his fantasies were filled with aggression, so was his behavior when the restrictions of correctional institutions were no longer constraining him. He often lost reality contact when in pursuit of his impulse gratification. This, of course, led to very poor judgment. This explained why he was so often caught in criminal activity as soon as he got back out into society.

According to all of the test results, Smith was a very dangerous, sociopathic individual who had no feelings for the rights and feelings of other people. One report recommended that Smith should not be released through any method beyond the expiration of his sentence. He was deemed to be an extremely dangerous individual who should remain incarcerated in a maximum-security institution until there was absolutely no doubt that he would be incapable of physical aggression upon other people and also unable to take advantage of other people through his criminal glibness.

In 1974, Smith scored an IQ of 117, which was only 4 points higher than the IQ he had achieved ten years earlier on the same test. However, there was only a one-point difference in the two tests as far as the performance IQ is concerned. This indicated that there had been very little change in Smith's ability for work, work planning, and control of his behavior.

The big change in Smith had come on the verbal parts of the test. The large jump (seven points) in his verbal ability indicated that he had become a more skillful, manipulative verbally oriented psychopath. He had simply added to his skills of manipulating other people on a verbal level. No other skills appeared to have been improved during the 10-year period. The reports painted a clear picture of a skillful manipulator, and one counselor even noted that Smith is so effective at convincing his superiors of his goodness when incarcerated that he is often easily transferred to positions of lesser security.

Chapter 6: Smith's Criminal History– The Recidivist

In the course of my preparation for trial, I thought it would be important to have the full institutional records on Smith. I felt all along that he was keeping a lot of things back from me, not only about the crime itself, but also about his background. So, I issued a Subpoena Duces Tecum (a request to bring a document or exhibit to court) and, finally, on the first day of the trial, a penitentiary guard approached me with all the institutional records on Smith. He refused to release them to me, however. Per policy, the guard would have to stay with the records the entire duration of the trial.

This wasn't the first time I had wrestled over records in a courtroom. There were at least 2,000 pages in this file, and things were hectic during the first several days of the trial. I couldn't get to those records immediately. The officer did, in fact, remain for two weeks, but finally decided it would be easier to copy the entire file rather than waste a whole month in court protecting them.

When I was finally able to wade through each entry, I further realized just how dangerous and clever Smith was. Smith's criminal record had started early in life, and the pattern was clear. He simply could not keep out of trouble in free society. His records showed that this trait was identified while he was incarcerated in

1964—almost nine years before the killing of Martin. Over time, he had just grown more dangerous and violent.

On September 13, 1967, a sergeant wrote a report to the assistant warden of custody at the Maryland House of Correction. It stated, on that date "... Smith approached me as I entered the sewing shop and requested that I check him in. I proceeded to ask him what reason he had for wanting to be checked in. He handed me a letter which he himself had written naming inmates who [sic] he had dealings with that he owed money to and that were threatening his life. Smith was placed on the segregation tier for protective custody."

The letter Smith had written was also contained in the file. It made interesting reading, as it gave an inside view of life in a major penal institution. It was titled "To whom I give this to."

> *Upon my arrival at the Penitentiary in May of 1964, I was approached by Arnold Zozzy (before I was assigned to a job) and asked if I wanted a clerk's in the storeroom, I said yes and a short while later I was assigned to work for Mr. Deeks, in the storeroom as his clerk. Zozzy asked me to type up some pool tickets for him, I did because he had pull and besides I owed him for the Job. He would keep a stock of cigarettes in my file cabinet that was used for this pool. One day he got hit big (I don't know the exact amount, but it was so much, he didn't have enough), so he came to me and said he knew a fellow that would lend me a hundred dollars in cash on his say so. He said the reason he didn't want to ask him for himself was because he didn't want this fellow to know he didn't have the backing to pay off. He said he would tell his fellow (whose name is Robert Roberts) that I had a source to buy some kind of pills and needed the money for a couple of weeks, and that I would pay interest on his money. This one was to be given to me in a couple of weeks by Zozzy to pay Roberts back. The week for the payoff arrived and Zozzy kept stalling and I didn't know what to do, so he told me not to worry that another guy would lend me the interest and by that time Zozzy was supposed to have all the money*

to pay up everything. The money came from a fellow who left on Saturday (John Oden). I was told at this time not to ever say a thing about cash or this transaction. About five days after receiving the money from Oden, Captain Alvey called me to this office and asked if I had a way of getting any money. I told him no and asked why. He told me he knew that I owed money and that he had to lock me up to protect me or that I would be killed. I denied owing anything (big mistake) but I was placed on segregation in August of 1964. Zozzy pretended that he didn't know me and these two guys Roberts and Oden wouldn't listen to anything. They swore to kill me. I told no one of this until now because I am forced to. I stayed on segregation until January 1967 when I was transferred here. After twenty-nine months of segregation for something that technically I was innocent of and couldn't explain to anyone was a terrible ordeal. When I came home I was happy. I was assigned as a clerk in the sewing shop (where I still am). Mr. Galkas was verifying what a worker I am. I work and go to my quarters and that's all. I get along with everybody then bang, John Oden came here. He sent word to me while I was in the hospital to get his money. To make a long story short I borrowed from this man and that man to get him paid. Then borrowed from others to pay others. I have had nothing from my commissary and the money from the test I am on. I just paid out every week. But with interest and all, it got so big that I can't pay, so now I am in worse shape than ever. In fact some of it was to be paid in cash so that a supply of pills or whatever it is they use could be brought. I got myself into this by fear and wish I would never have met Zozzy or associated with anyone. I don't bother anybody but I can't sleep at night from worry. Now everyone is expecting their money Thursday and Friday. I just don't have it. So lock up is the only place. Although I will even fear that because I was told I could be got to even there, number of ways. So I don't know what to do. I sure can't disclose the names of the men. This is all true.

Signed,
James F. Smith

The file also revealed that Smith had been numbered early in life by the F.B.I. as "2 523 215." Just a short glance revealed that he had made crime his livelihood. The file included numerous known arrests, starting in 1941, when Smith was just 19.

- In Cumberland, Maryland, on May 22, 1941, Smith was investigated for false pretenses and released. In Pittsburgh, Pennsylvania, he was detained at the Allegany County Jail on November 22, 1941, for embezzlement. He was also charged in two other cases for false pretenses. He took a plea to one of them and was given a year's probation.

- In Pittsburgh, Pennsylvania, on May 28, 1942, he was arrested for assault and robbery, and two weeks later, on June 12, he was charged with another robbery. On October 31, 1942, Smith entered pleas to the robbery and receiving stolen goods and received a sentence of 2 to 10 years. He was paroled on June 17, 1944.

- Smith violated his parole on June 21, 1946, by issuing worthless checks and was charged and found guilty. On July 2, 1946, he was approved for parole and then released on October 14.

- In Allegany County, Pennsylvania, Smith was arrested on four cases of false pretenses and four cases of larceny by trick on June 27, 1947 and December 2, 1947. He was given a two-year sentence for these crimes. Smith served 19 months and was discharged in January of 1949. A few days later, however, he violated parole and was forced to serve the balance of his sentence.

- In Little Rock, Arkansas, on Christmas 1952, Smith was, once again, charged with false pretenses. A week later, more charges of forging and uttering were entered against him. He had to wait until April 6 before these charges came before a court, at which time, he received a sentence of five years.

- On March 4, 1958, Smith was given another sentence of two to four years for larceny by trick, and just a couple of days later, seven more larceny by trick, cheating by fraud, and pretense charges were placed against him in Pittsburgh. On March 11, 1958, he escaped and became a fugitive. On March 24, while a fugitive, Smith was arrested for assault and battery with intent to ravish in Pittsburgh, Pennsylvania, but was mistakenly released.

- Several months later, on October 17, Smith was, once again, arrested in Allegheny County. This time, the charges were for larceny by trick and attempted larceny by trick. A month later, on November 14, he was fined $100 and received four years' incarceration. The past charges were also brought against him at that time, and he received two to four years, with the time to be run concurrently.

- In Allegany County, Pittsburgh, Pennsylvania, on December 8, 1962, he was held for the district attorney for investigation for homicide. He was detained several weeks but was released without trial.

- On May 17, 1963, Smith was arrested in Baltimore, Maryland, under the alias James Francis Bell for larceny by trick. He was charged again, on November 22, 1963, in Towson, Maryland, for false pretenses. He awaited trial until May 25, 1965, when he received a 10-year sentence.

- In Annapolis, Maryland, on September 22, 1969, Smith was charged with armed robbery. He was given a 12-year sentence.

Wisely, institutions have dictated that all non-legal incoming and outgoing mail of inmates should be copied and placed in the base file. This gives the officials an overview on the activities of inmates while they are in the detention center. The records reveal not only the dates and times of visitors, but also the number of incoming letters they receive.

Smith's file had a good amount of personal correspondence, and it shocked me, since it revealed that Smith had received at least three letters a week from Buffington for several months. She was in love!

The file also revealed a few other interesting kernels of information. Under Smith's 10-year sentence for false pretenses in Baltimore County, he should have been incarcerated from May 25, 1964 through May 20, 1976. (This was longer than 10 years because Smith had to serve the balance of his previous sentence—since he had violated his parole—before starting the latest sentence.) However, on October 25, 1968, Smith cooperated with police and authorities at the Maryland House of Correction regarding alleged charges against employees, and thus managed to be paroled, once again, in March of 1969—seven years early. Smith then found work as a medical aid at the Anne Arundel General Hospital. He was successful on the job and received pay raises.

The report revealed another surprising fact: Smith had gotten married for the third time on July 26, 1969. His bride was Mary Lou Mullins of Annapolis, a divorced 38-year-old woman. This relationship began in April and quickly developed into a marriage. She and Smith made their home in a rented apartment that Smith obtained. Reliable information revealed that Smith had borrowed $1,500 from his new mother-in-law to finance the wedding and reception. By the time of my reading, Mary Lou Mullins had advised that she intended to divorce Smith.

During his parole in 1969, Smith had been taking part in several high stakes gambling games and finally admitted that he had lost approximately $1,100. He claimed he was reprimanded and advised that his continued parole depended on adherence to the parole rules. Smith continued to work for the Anne Arundel

General Hospital, and his wages soon increased to $1.86 per hour. He also started to work as a waiter approximately three nights a week at the Statler Hilton Hotel where he made between $20 and $25 a night in tips. But, that all came to an end on September 26, 1969, when Major Kalnoske of the Annapolis City Police arrested Smith for the armed robbery of Aspasia Nicholas.

The method of perpetration was, once again, a confidence game. On August 28, 1969, Smith called Nicholas on the telephone, told her about a "friend" who needed a room, and then showed up himself to take the room. He paid a deposit and was given a key. He happened to see Nicholas putting money in her pocketbook during his visit. When he returned later that night, he grabbed her from the back, placed a knife at her throat and bound and gagged her. He attempted to put her in a downstairs closet, but there was not enough room. So, Smith took Nicholas upstairs where he put a pocket handkerchief inside her mouth and tied another one around it. He threw her on the bed, climbed on top of her, sodomized her, and put his hand over her nose for several minutes during the process.

Eventually, Smith threatened to kill Nicholas if she reported the crime and left the room, went downstairs, and took $800 from an envelope in her pocketbook. When Nicholas initially reported the crime, she made no mention of the rape, likely out of a feeling of intense shame, as is common in cases of sexual assault. Although that part of the attack eventually came to light, it was not included in the charges.

Smith vehemently denied his guilt and insisted that he has been working when the offense took place; however, Nicholas positively identified Smith.

When he was arrested, Smith had a newspaper clipping in his possession. It contained advertisements for rooms for rent.

Apparently, Smith had also pulled a similar con game recently in Cumberland, Maryland, where he took $600 from a landlady. He had not been arrested on this charge, but the police were making arrangements for an identification lineup. A retake warrant was issued for Smith, so he could be placed in the detention center he had been paroled from.

Most of Smith's life had been divided between criminal activities and institutionalization. In the file, one counselor concluded that Smith had a lengthy criminal record and had to be considered a recidivist who could not learn from past experience. The counselor further noted that Smith had been unsuccessful on parole and was a practiced liar and con man who revealed how dangerous he could be by the tactics in his present offense. It was based partly upon this report that Judge Evans gave Smith a 12-year sentence for the armed robbery of Nicholas. It should be noted, however, that 12 years was inexplicably not the maximum that could have been given. Once again, Smith had prevailed. If he had been given the maximum sentences for his crimes throughout his life—and made to serve them—many innocent people could have been saved.

By now, there could be no doubt that Smith was an imminent threat to society.

Chapter 7:
A Glimpse into Smith's Prison Life

Smith was good at working the system. He had a high verbal IQ, which allowed him to be a deft manipulator. He understood the system and was good at making it work for him. Smith was able to make the right impression on many key people (although not everyone was fooled). He routinely ran betting pools in prison, which earned him money and favor with some inmates but got him in trouble with others.

Prisoners in maximum security prisons can earn good conduct time (GCT), and there are several types of GCT. By statute, some GCT credit is awarded based purely on the length of time that a prisoner is incarcerated with no incident. For example, if you go six months without any sort of write-up, you get GCT credits. These credits are mandatory and, once earned, generally cannot be revoked. Some time is also earned when a prisoner works and receiving a good on the spot report can result in GCT as well.

Smith knew how to behave and who to behave in front of. He became a master of good "on-the-spot reports." He would act friendly, responsible, and even jovial with certain prison officials when he knew they could help him. For example, he'd work particularly hard in the kitchen one day, then strike up a conversation with the nearest officer—maybe ask him about his kids or his wife. Then, he'd request a complimentary on-the-spot report. One report here, one report there; they added up to years taken off Smith's sentences.

Smith's letter writing played a part as well. His relentless letter-writing campaigns to officials containing requests for good recommendations became an effective tool in getting him what he wanted.

At one point in Smith's tenure at the Maryland House of Correction, he approached a correctional officer and asked to be put on lockup for his own protection, as he owed another inmate money (from his baseball pool). While in confinement on segregation, even for his own protection, Smith could not earn money or GCT. So, he used his connections to the prison grapevine and made use of his letter-writing habit to get a job.

Warden John Garrity knew Smith well and was used to receiving letters from him every couple of days, begging for stamps or toothpaste, cigarettes, and even money for essentials. Smith was always extremely polite in these letters and had figured out that if he bothered the warden enough, one request out of every seven or eight would usually be granted. Such was the case when Smith requested the tier runner job he had heard would soon be vacant. This allowed Smith to continue to earn GCT—even while being in protective lockup, which had resulted from him conducting illegal betting pools.

A parole hearing summary is written by a committee made up of an inmate's correctional classification officer and supervisor with the advice of a psychologist and information from psychological/psychiatric reports. The warden has an opportunity to concur with the opinion of the committee.

In preparation for Smith's parole hearing date on November 2, 1965, Mr. M.J. Traurig wrote a parole hearing summary. The report stated that, since admission, Smith was employed in the central storeroom, where he earned satisfactory work grades. It mentioned that Smith was placed in segregation for being involved in a gambling pool, and he was presently there. Due to the subject's short amount of time at the facility, and the fact that most of that time was spent in segregation, Smith had not partaken in any institutional groups or activities. The summary indicated that his overall adjustment was "satisfactory."

However, since Smith's criminal record began as far back as 1942, ran to the present, and included very little time in free society, the committee recommended that Smith must be considered a recidivist who cannot learn from past experience, and the counselor advised that Smith not be granted parole. The classification supervisor, Leo Davidson, agreed. Parole was denied, and a new hearing was scheduled for February 1969.

When February 1969 came around, a new classification counselor, Michael D. Vander, came to a different conclusion. The acting warden of the Maryland House of Correction stated that Smith cooperated with police and authorities at the institution regarding alleged charges against employees. His cooperation enabled the institution to resolve problems it was having concerning those employees. As a result, Vander interviewed Smith and accepted a parole plan from him.

Vander attached letters of verification to the parole hearing summary indicating that, if paroled, Smith would work at the Anne Arundel General Hospital in Annapolis, Maryland. Smith had acceptable temporary housing lined up until he could find something permanent and Vander recommended that Smith be paroled.

In the summary, under the evaluation and recommendation sections, this new, obviously green counselor wrote:

> *... my first contact with this man was on February 21, 1969 when I interviewed him in regard to his parole hearing at the Detention Center (3 days before his parole hearing on the 24th of February, 1969). Recommendation will be made on the basis of my first interview with the subject. Smith has a parole plan which is being completed with the assistance of many people. His institutional adjustment since being at the Detention Center has resulted in praise by all those associated with him. Therefore, it is my recommendation that parole at this time be granted to this man who is now 46 years of age and realizes that he must now decide whether he is going to accept living in society or spend the rest of his life in penal institutions.*

It is astounding to know that, on the basis of this one interview with Smith, this classification counselor recommended parole, notwithstanding Smith's already voluminous institutional and criminal record. Even more shocking is the fact that it was Leo Davidson who signed the recommendation for parole. Just months later, Smith would wind up robbing and raping Aspasia Nichols.

In 1972, after serving approximately two years after returning to prison for the Nichols crime, Smith was transferred from the Food Service Department at Maryland Correctional Training Center to the Work Release Center, where he was allowed to work on an outside detail for the Food Service Department. On July 3, 1972, he was transferred to the work release program where he obtained a job with the Sheraton Motor Inn in Hagerstown, Maryland.

Just days later, the chief psychologist at the Maryland House of Correction in Hagerstown saw Smith and recommended that he continue in the work release program.

On October 19, approximately three months after Smith was placed at the Sheraton Motor Inn, the manager filed a complaint that Smith was involved in matters with his employees that involved a considerable amount of money. Apparently, Smith was gambling heavily on horses and in football pools, and he owed quite a bit of money to his coworkers. On a series of consecutive days in October, he attempted to borrow money from several different waitresses, each time asking for hundreds of dollars and promising hundreds more upon return. On October 18, he called one waitress at her home on an unlisted telephone number, which he presumably got from sneaking a look at the office file. He told her that he had raised $550 and asked her to lend him only $150. The manager expressed that the waitresses were all frightened that Smith would kill them if they told, and no one was willing to come forward. Smith was removed from the work release program and sent back to the correctional institution.

He appeared to make a very good adjustment upon his return. Just a few months later, on January 10, 1973, Smith received a positive on-the-spot report from Correctional Officer G.S. Beck. "This man is the food service clerk and he also voluntarily helps in the staff kitchen when the need arrives, and he has an overall knowledge of the Department and needs no supervision. His work is of the excellent caliber and anything that he does is done with a mature attitude." Beck further stated that work release consideration would certainly be warranted.

On January 25, 1973, Correctional Officer Beals wrote:

> ... it is my judgement that outside classification should be given Mr. Smith. His institutional adjustment and work record have been more than satisfactory and denial of work release to date is sufficient punishment for his indiscretion on his work release. This man is 49 years old. He has been incarcerated on the present sentence since 9/25/69 and there is a possibility that his fiancé may be responsible more than any other factor for rehabilitation. I would be in favor of reconsideration for work release four or five months prior to his August 1973 parole hearing.

However, the classification board recommended that Smith's assignment not be changed, and that his requests for work release and outside classification both be denied.

Smith also wrote to Superintendent Paul Wagley at the Maryland Camp Training Center, on January 28, 1973, seeking further consideration.

> I just hope I am not making a bad fellow out of myself by me continually contacting you. I realize that you are a busy man and have so many other things to take care of. However, please try to understand my personal problems. When you evaluated the recent majority vote of the three-man panel I was before on the 25th, I would like you to know of one very important factor that you will not find in the record. As you know prior to almost four years ago, I have a terrible record, but in the past almost four years I have found something that I have never had in my entire life. Love. There is a woman and three wonderful boys out there that love me, and I love them. My only desire in the world is to live out the rest of my life

enjoying them, and to receive all the wonderful benefits of a happy family life. I could write anything, Mr. Wagley, and you couldn't know if I was truly sincere or not—only my future actions will tell.

What I need is a friend to take the chance and give me the benefit of the doubt, by helping me to do what I so much want to do. To work out and help to support my family since it is needed very much. I promise you with all my heart you will never regret giving me your help. When I am finally released I will be living just five minutes away on Garris Road. From time to time I will come in contact with some of the officers here that is either going to or coming from work. I know if I am ever brought up in a conversation it will be something like, "saw Smith mowing his lawn, stopped to say hello, he is doing very good." Whatever help you give me—you will never be forgotten. Thank you.

*Sincerely,
James Smith*

Wagley, however, was all-too-familiar with Smith's calculations. He wrote back on February 2, 1973:

You were approved for minimum classification when last seen by the Classification Team. However, you were not approved for transfer to another correctional camp system. I believe this to be appropriate in that your fiancé is living in this area after having moved from Baltimore to be near you, and I do not believe that it would be advantageous for you to be transferred to the Camp Center. I have instructed the Classification Department to have you brought before the Team for consideration for work release again in the Hagerstown area in April 1973. I am not promising that you will be approved at that time, only that you will be considered.

Wagley did not like the idea that Buffington had moved to Hagerstown to be near Smith, and he was now requesting to be transferred to the Camp Center in Jessup. Wagley felt that Smith should remain in the Hagerstown area close to her if she was, in fact, a positive force in his life. Nevertheless, in March 1973, Smith was approved for family leave for a weekend. He was required to sign an acceptance to the minimum leave plan, which was explained to him, and he agreed to comply with all its terms and conditions. Buffington was also sent a weekend leave notification explaining that Smith was to be met by her, at the institution, on March 23 and returned on March 25, 1973, no later than 10 p.m. Buffington was told that only she was authorized to pick up Smith and any other person coming to pick him up would cause the leave to be cancelled.

Having successfully complied with these terms, Smith impressed some of his immediate officers and supervisors. A positive on-the-spot report was written on his behalf by Officer Myer Broom on April 4, 1973:

Smith has worked for me as a clerk for five months; I feel he is an outstanding resident as far as his attitude towards his job, his incarceration and his prospect for the future. He will perform any indoor task assigned to him and help where ever needed even as a cook. I feel Smith is on his way to a better life, and should be given consideration for possibly an earlier parole hearing.

On April 10, 1973, the committee considered Smith's request for placement in the work release program in Hagerstown. Three of the committee members decided that Smith should be placed on the program at that time. One officer, Bliss, did not concur. In addition, Wagley, when shown the recommendation wrote that "no decision was necessary from [him], but [he] disagreed with the majority."

This was the decision that allowed Smith to participate in the work release program in November 1973.

Chapter 8: The Trial, Part I

The trial was set for Monday, July 8, 1974, before Judge James Perrott. I was nervous when I entered the judge's chambers with a group that included the prosecutors Mark Kolman and Gary Jordan. I found myself feeling sorry for the judge—whom I had known for several years—because I knew the amount of work that the case was going to entail for us all.

The first thing I did was move to dismiss the case pursuant to the Intrastate Detainer Act[6] that required that new charges against an inmate be tried within 120 days. The only exception to this 120-day period of limitation was "for good cause."

The state did not contest that the request for prompt disposition had been properly made or even that more than 120 days had since elapsed. Rather, the state argued that Smith had effectively waived his rights at his arraignment and that good cause had, indeed, been shown for a continuance granted during the 120-day period. The limitation period began to run on February 22, 1974, and expired on June 22, 1974. When the case was called for trial, 136 days had elapsed.

Perrott assumed that Smith had not effectively waived his rights under the statute, and he ruled that the continuance granted on April 11, 1974, had been for "good cause"—namely, to allow a psychiatric examination of Smith and to allow the defense more

Room for Rent

time to prepare for trial. And, so, we proceeded with a trial on the merits and began with jury selection.

It's always a grand moment when the jury has been selected, and the judge directs the prosecutor to make his or her opening statement. It's said that 80 percent of criminal cases are won in the opening statement. So, even if the defense attorney doesn't know what he is going to say or what his defense is going to be, it is critical that he get up and, at the very least, make his presence known after the prosecution has finished.

It is always easy for the prosecutor to make an opening statement because he has a case; it's easy to make a succinct prediction about what the witnesses and exhibits will reveal. But, when the defense attorney rises, he must be very careful. Anything he says is going to be hurled back at him in closing argument. He can't overpromise, and he has to be very careful about what he commits to because, if he doesn't fulfill his commitment, it gives the prosecutor a whole line of argument in closing.

However, the defense attorney still must get into the case fists and feet. He has to get his personality into the case to keep the jurors interested in the defense table. Otherwise, they're not going to hear from him until he starts cross examining witnesses. And cross examination is always confrontational, so if you don't make a good impression in the opening, the jury will get its first look at you as being tricky, obstructionist, aggressive, etc. It is much better to spend 10 or 15 minutes (or more) in the opening statement letting the jurors see, in part, who you are.

One of the arts of defense is to try to distract and to lighten the atmosphere. If a defense attorney is clever and has at his command, pithy, witty little comments he can make, it's a tremendous advantage. However, it's a two-edge sword. If you are just there to show off how clever you are, you are no doubt going to be disliked by the jurors, and they are going to believe you are just a callous, cynical lawyer. So, it has got to be done very delicately. You can only make humorous comments when they are appropriate. If you have the ability to do that, that is what you are trying to do

---

6. Maryland Code (1957, 1972 Repl. Vol.), Article 27, section 61S

all the time; you are trying to lighten the atmosphere. Clarence Darrow said no juror has ever decided to execute someone if they have been laughing in the jury box. In this case, it was extremely hard to come up with any light moments. But, there were a few.

In my opening, I tried to inoculate the jury against what they were going to hear about the kind of man Smith was by presenting the information myself.

Like most trials, this one started off slowly after the opening statements. Everyone is always intrigued by the first witnesses and they tend to take a lot more time. As the days go by, people are less interested in the detail during the direct examination and are getting tired of watching the defense attorney attack every witness. It becomes transparent that the defense attorney is a glorified attack dog. His attacks must be done artfully, so the jury will still like him as much as possible.

The prosecution produced 15 witnesses during the first two weeks of the trial, and they presented a textbook case: the responding officer who secured the murder scene, the medical examiner who performed the autopsy, the detectives who investigated the case. They were perfunctory witnesses, but nevertheless extremely compelling, and they offered fact after fact of circumstantial evidence.

Officer Slawinski started his testimony by describing how he was on patrol when he received a call to investigate a death in Hampden. Upon arrival, he told the jury, he proceeded to a second-floor bedroom where he found the victim, later identified as Doris Martin. He described how he found her: on the bed beneath a blanket, lying face down on her stomach in a diagonal position on the bed. He described how there were blood stains splattered on the headboard, walls, curtains, and bureau. Slawinski further relayed that Martin had sustained a "large head wound," and there were apparent stab wounds in her back. He vividly painted the picture of Martin, with her hands tied behind her back and twisted so that her left arm was at an approximate 90-degree angle and her right arm at a 45-degree angle. The jury was enrapt.

Dr. Craig Duncan, assistant medical examiner for the state of Maryland, then corroborated Slawinski's testimony on Martin's general condition. He noted his opinion that the victim died sometime between 5 p.m., November 12, 1973 and 5 a.m., November 13, 1973.

Duncan continued, telling the jury that he performed an autopsy on November 14, 1973. He noted that Martin's blood group was Type A Positive. He also noted, for what would be the second time in his testimony, that Martin had sustained a massive head injury, which was evidenced by a large 4-inch by one-half-inch laceration to the right side of the head and two smaller scalp lacerations. He gave further detail: underlying this was a major fracture of the skull, extending into the vicinity of the right eye as well as a brain injury. Martin also had a black eye and prominent bruising of both lips with a loosening of the lower middle teeth, compatible with a blow or impact to the face. In addition, Duncan discussed the number of stab wounds Martin sustained to the lower left back. He explained that two wounds entered significantly into the body, penetrating the left lung and causing hemorrhaging. Duncan was of the opinion that the cause of death was the sum of four deep stab wounds and the blunt force injury to the head, resulting in the skull fracture. Either the stab wounds or the head injuries alone would have been sufficient to cause death.

Whitney, the crime lab technician, testified that he responded to the crime scene on the day in question and took photographs, dusted for latent fingerprints, and preserved physical evidence. He lifted three latent prints from the kitchen cabinet doors, but they were later found to be unsuitable for comparison. Remarkably, no other prints were found in the house. In addition, Whitney testified that he took blood scrapings from Martin's bedroom wall and recovered a pink face towel that was soaked in blood.

Detective Russell noted there were no signs of forced entry other than the bathroom window that had been opened by the neighbors. Russell also corroborated the testimonies of Slawinski and Duncan as to the general condition of Martin's body and the house and told the jury about the note he found next to the telephone in the living room. The jury was informed that the FBI crime lab handwriting expert determined that the note was written by Martin.

Russell then talked about his unsuccessful search for weapons. He noted that a drawer in the kitchen, containing utensils, was pulled out and almost completely falling out of the cabinet. He informed the jury that he and Chuck Herring, a crime lab technician, returned to the premises for a subsequent search. At that time, he observed a brick that was up against the door to the entrance of the kitchen. The brick appeared to have blood and some other type of matter on it.

Russell then addressed his trip to Hagerstown to interview Buffington, informing the jury about the boxes of clothing and toiletries Smith had sent her. Russell then identified, in court, the suit pants and jacket found in those boxes. In addition, he mentioned one of the boxes contained several classified ads from *The Baltimore Sun*, all featuring rooms and apartments for rent and help wanted ads. The blue suit jacket that appeared to have blood splattered on the right side of it was shown to the jury. Later, Robert Davis, a lab technician, testified that both the jacket and the brick were stained with human blood, Type A—compatible with Martin's blood type.

Several neighbors testified to activity near Martin's home on November 12 and 13. Notably, Esther Johnson testified that she saw Martin walking her dog around 6:30 or 7 p.m. on November 12, and Katherine Hackley testified that Martin called her at 4:10 p.m. on November 12. Hackley further testified that she saw a light go on in the victim's living room between 5 and 6 p.m., then saw a light go on briefly in the front room on the second floor and saw someone walk across that room. Afterward, a light went on again for 5 or 10 minutes in the upstairs front bedroom. Hackley stated that she called the victim at 9:30 p.m. and again 10 minutes later but got no answer.

The state showed that Martin had advertised a furnished room for rent in *The Baltimore Sun* newspaper on November 11 and 12, 1973, reading, "Hampden—Employed refined gent. No drinking or smoking. 889-6769."

The prosecutors informed the jury that the detectives found a copy of that newspaper, with the ad marked in red, in a box of Smith's possessions, and they dramatically introduced it into evidence.

Cherita Bishop, a barmaid from the Keg of Ale Restaurant in Baltimore City, testified next. According to her testimony, she saw Smith in the restaurant on November 12. He was wearing a blue suit jacket and arrived around 8:30 p.m. He was joined by a second man around 9:15 p.m., and the two left together around 9:55 p.m. Bishop testified that she had a conversation with Smith in which he told her that he used to live in Pittsburgh and that he worked for the baby food division of H.J. Heinz Company.

The state elicited testimony from Buffington that Smith had a preference for Heinz pickles and ketchup, which Smith had explained by the fact that Heinz was a Pittsburgh, Pennsylvania, company, and Smith was brought up in a suburb of Pittsburgh.

Perkowski and Russell both testified that Smith was brought to the Homicide Office at Central Police Headquarters in the late afternoon of December 18, 1973. Smith was told that they were investigating the homicide of Doris Martin. Perkowski read Smith his Miranda rights and had him sign the explanation of rights form. The detectives testified that no one exerted any threats, coercion, promises, or improper influence upon Smith, and that Smith indicated a willingness to discuss the matter with them and did not indicate a desire to have an attorney present. During the course of an interview that extended approximately five hours, Smith demonstrated some awareness of the facts surrounding the crime, mentioning that the victim had had a room for rent stating, "... I didn't stab her anyway." Smith denied any knowledge whatsoever of the crime, yet neither the fact of the room rental nor the fact of the stabbing had been previously revealed by the detectives. According to Perkowski's notes, corroborated by Russell's statement, the following exchange also took place at this interview:

Question: James, do we have the right man? Do you have the courage to tell us the truth? If you killed her, say so; no one is going to hurt you.

Answer: I'm sorry I did it, but I'll never admit it and I'll never say anything. If you say I admitted it, I'll deny it later.

The prosecutors then put on several other would-be victims that Smith had tried to flimflam in the days preceding the murder. Things were not looking good.

Compelling as it was, however, the state's evidence did not go undisputed.

As a general rule, I have excellent control over my clients. I have a good working relationship with them, and I can count on them to trust my professional advice. However, this was decidedly not the case with Smith. As I've mentioned, we never connected—despite my best attempts and my habit of trying to personalize him by calling him "Jimmie." His calculated attempt from the very beginning to set me up as incompetent for a post-conviction appeal was just one part of the reason.

Another part was that I could not find anything in him that I would label as humanity. I had learned over the years that most humans can relate to each other through humor, and this part of my personality played a large part in my success. But there was not even an ounce of humor in Smith. This made it difficult for me to humanize him. This was a problem, not only for me, but I knew it would also be problematic for the jury.

For that reason, I felt strongly that Smith should not testify at his trial. Nevertheless, as a result of his profound hubris, he insisted. He thought he would win the jury over the same way he was inexplicably able to win over so many other people in his life. This turned out to be a dismal failure.

One of the most difficult parts of the case was when Smith was on the witness stand. I had to hide the tension between us from the jurors. It was critical, if he were to have any chance at all, that they believe that I liked him, that I was not scared of him, and that I felt he was innocent. To do that, it's necessary to touch defendants from time to time, a gesture like putting your arm around them to convey a kind of closeness—but I didn't like touching Smith. On the couple of occasions when I did put my hand on his shoulder, I felt dirty. He was a chain smoker, his fingers were permanently yellow from nicotine, and he had a body odor that I didn't enjoy being near.

I did my best to keep a straight face and appear to the jurors to believe every word Smith said. He was a good liar because he was so confident about his ability to deceive, but he did not make a good witness because of his lack of humanity. I glanced over at the jurors frequently, trying to read their faces. And, if I had to guess, I'd say it was pretty obvious that they hated the son of a bitch.

Smith vehemently denied any involvement in Martin's murder, and he had an impassioned rebuttal for some of what the state presented. He testified that the Type A blood got on his suit jacket as the result of a fight he had with another inmate in October 1973. Smith acknowledged that he had previously told Perkowski and Russell that the blood was his own, the result of a nosebleed, explaining that he had lied so as not to implicate himself or the other inmate in a violation of a no-fighting rule that would result in a loss of privileges.

He denied agreeing to talk to the detectives without a lawyer present, and he denied having confessed to the crime. But, the meat of Smith's testimony revolved around his self-proclaimed "alibi defense"—his claim that he could not have murdered Martin since he was in Alexandria at the time, committing larceny.

In order to fully explain this alibi, Smith testified about much of his background. He revealed to the jury that he had been convicted of numerous crimes, mostly involving false pretenses. He admitted that he began using a confidence game or "flimflam" in the early 1960s. With minor variations, he explained, the operation worked as follows:

Smith would call one or more numbers listed in the newspaper classifieds, advertising a furnished room for rent. On reaching a good prospect, almost always a woman, Smith would impersonate a "Mr. Pierson," a supervisor at some well-known company, seeking a room for a "Mr. Bell," one of his employees due to arrive in town later that day. "Mr. Pierson" would offer several dollars more than the asking price, explaining that the company allowed "Mr. Bell" the higher figure as the normal living expense. "Mr. Pierson" would then tell the woman that he was leaving shortly on a flight to Chicago, but that he would leave word for "Mr. Bell" to call her and make arrangements to move in if the woman could hold the room for an hour or two. "Mr. Pierson" would then ask the woman to give "Mr. Bell" the message that he was leaving town, and he would forward "Mr. Bell's" bonus check of several thousand dollars to the woman's address when he arrived in Chicago.

Smith would wait about 45 minutes and then, disguising his voice, call as "Mr. Bell." Arriving at the home, "Mr. Bell" would praise the woman's housekeeping, otherwise flatter her, and profess to be delighted with the room. When given the message about the bonus check, "Mr. Bell" would become depressed and worried (sometimes saying his wallet had been stolen) and say he needed some amount of money—usually a few hundred dollars—of that check to get his personal belongings from the train station. The woman would then offer to lend him the money until the check arrived. Smith would accept gratefully and never be seen again.

Smith told the jury he answered Buffington's ad for a room for rent in 1969 but did not go through with his con because he fell in love with her. At the time, she was separated from her husband and had three sons. She and Smith developed a close relationship that continued when Smith was incarcerated several months later. Buffington wrote to him daily and visited him every Saturday and Sunday. When travel between Lutherville and the prison in Hagerstown became burdensome, Buffington sold her house and moved to Hagerstown with her children. Smith described their relationship as "common-law husband and wife" and said they planned to be married when Smith was released from his 12-year sentence (Buffington corroborated this when she later took the stand). Smith also testified that his life changed because of his relationship with Buffington and her sons.

Smith continued to describe his background for the jury. In December 1970, he was transferred to the minimum-security prison in Hagerstown where he learned to be a cook. By the summer of 1973, he had qualified for a state job as a dietary officer and, in August of that year, he was denied parole but recommended for the work release program. The next month, he was transferred to the Maryland Correctional Training Center (MCTC), another state prison facility located in Hagerstown, where he worked as a cook in the officer's dining room.

During the first week of October, Smith told the jury, he was approached at MCTC by a man who introduced himself as Mr. Andretti. Andretti had a folder containing Smith's institutional records and offered to arrange a Christmas commutation for him by the governor for $5,000. The terms would be: $200 for the initial paperwork, $800 by November, and the balance of $4,000 within a year of Smith's release. The commutation would be worked out secretly and Smith was to act completely surprised when the commutation was awarded. He should never, of course, mention Andretti. Smith agreed and paid Andretti the first $200, most of which he obtained from Buffington.

Soon thereafter, Smith was transferred to the Maryland Correctional Camp Center in Jessup, where he was assigned to the kitchen. Smith made numerous attempts to obtain a work release job on the outside, so he could earn the rest of the money for Andretti. His attempts were eventually successful, and, on November 6, 1973, Smith signed a work release form to begin as a cook at Emerson's Restaurant in Baltimore City. He was to work the 4 p.m. to midnight shift. The Camp Center bus for inmates on work release routinely left the prison between 2 and 2:30 p.m. and arrived in Baltimore between 3 and 3:30 p.m. The inmates picked up the return bus at the Maryland Rehabilitation Center on Greenmount Avenue between 11 p.m. and midnight and were then returned to the prison.

Smith testified that he took the bus into Baltimore on November 7 for his first day of work, but when he arrived at Emerson's, the manager informed him the position had been rejected by the work release authorities because it was not permanent. He spent the rest of the day applying for jobs in other restaurants in Baltimore. Because his name was inadvertently left on the transportation list after the job fell through, Smith was still able to leave the institution on the bus on Thursday, Friday, and Monday, November 12, of that week. (He was not allowed to leave on Saturday or Sunday, November 10 and 11, as he had not been scheduled to work on weekends).

Smith claimed that he spent that Wednesday, Thursday, and Friday (November 7–8) applying for jobs in restaurants, including Forty Fathoms, the Holiday Inn, and the Charcoal Hearth. On Thursday, November 8, he said he saw Andretti at the prison. According to Smith, Andretti told him that he was expecting to see him Monday in Baltimore to receive the next installment of $800. Buffington then came to the prison and gave Smith some money, but he was still $350 short. On November 12, Smith bought a copy of *The Washington Post* while he was still in Baltimore. He decided to obtain the remaining $350 by operating his flimflam in Washington, D.C., having rejected the idea of operating in Baltimore because his M.O. was known to the Baltimore police.

Smith continued his testimony, all the while speaking emphatically and intensely. He stated that he took the camp bus, arriving in Baltimore around 3:30 p.m. Andretti met him as he got off the bus, and they arranged to meet later that night, around 10 or 10:30 p.m., at the Keg of Ale. Smith then claimed to have gotten a Greyhound bus at 4:30 p.m. and arrived in D.C. at approximately 5:20 p.m.

Room for Rent

He claimed that he made several calls from the station before he landed on a good prospect: a Mrs. Virginia Sullivan in Alexandria, Virginia. Smith took a cab to her home, pulled a variation of the scheme described above, and obtained $360 from her. It was close to 8 p.m. when a cab returned him to the D.C. Greyhound station. He got a bus back to Baltimore, arrived about 10:30 p.m., changed clothes, and went to the Keg of Ale. He was wearing an orange-brown corduroy jacket, and he had stuffed Andretti's $800 into its lining.

The two stayed only briefly at the Keg of Ale. Two waitresses recognized Andretti and spoke to him before he suggested he and Smith go to a nearby restaurant called Harley's because he was expecting a call there. Once at Harley's, Andretti said he had to go to the car and get some papers, taking Smith's jacket with him to remove the money. He instructed Smith to answer the phone in case it was the call he was expecting. Several minutes went by before the phone rang. When Smith answered, Andretti was on the other end and told him the commutation was a fraud. Smith ran outside looking for Andretti but failed to find him. He then returned to the rehabilitation center via the camp bus and had been incarcerated ever since.

Smith's story was verified in its main points by institutional records and the testimonies of both Buffington and Sullivan. Buffington verified their relationship and indicated that Smith had told her about Andretti in August or September. Further, she confirmed that she had given Smith more than $200 for the cause.

By stipulation, it was shown that Sullivan had advertised a room for rent in *The Washington Post* on September 30, October 13, and November 9, 1973. Smith testified that he was shown the classified ad section of the November 9 edition of *The Washington Post* during the investigation by the Office of the Public Defender and he had told the investigator that he wasn't sure exactly which number he had called, but he had narrowed it to four or five. It was the investigation of those numbers that resulted in the location of Sullivan. Sullivan, however, was too ill to appear in court, so it became clear that the prosecutors, Smith, and I would have to go to Alexandria to depose her.

During our pre-trial investigation, Sullivan had failed to pick Smith out of photographs as the man who stole money from her. The pictures she was shown were all fairly old, though, and Smith looked considerably different now than he did in the photos. We were taking a big risk, but we had no real choice. His alibi defense was our only hope.

The day before we were scheduled to depose Sullivan, Smith stood up in court and handed the clerk an envelope. On the outside, he had written, "In c/o of Court, Part I, Honorable Judge James Perrott, presiding. Maybe open anytime upon arriving back from Alexandria, Virginia, in the presence of his honor, Mr. Keating and Mr. Coleman [sic]." It was signed with his initials: J.F.S.

I quickly motioned to the clerk to give me the envelope since I had no idea what was in it. (Another example of Smith working on his own.) I asked the court to bear with me for a few moments and read the contents. Inside was a single page that said, "July 23, 1974, the day before going to the home of Mrs. Sullivan." It also contained a diagram, above which was the ground plan of a house. It read, "Below is a rough diagram of the downstairs of Mrs. Sullivan's home upon entering the front door of her home. In order to get to the front door, you must first climb a long pair of steps leading to her front perch, then to the front door. The home is on a corner, a right turn can be made at the left side of her home. It is an uphill street, or it might be called an alley, as it is not wide. That is where the cab waited for me."

Under that writing, there was another diagram of an alley running north and south and an avenue running east and west. It was a house on the corner between those two streets. High steps were clearly marked, extending from the sidewalk to the front porch and a bedroom was noted on the diagram. Smith had placed a code of numbers throughout, marking the front door, and the stairway to the upstairs of Sullivan's bedroom. On the bottom of the page was written, "1, front door, 2, some room to the immediate left upon entering home leads to the side entrance or exits to the alley, 3 stairway to upstairs, corner room to the right"

Under that, Smith had written, "Compare this with Mr. Keating's and Mr. Coleman's [sic] description." That was all in this mysterious envelope. After I had looked at it very carefully, I wrote on the outside, "To be open at the request of the defendant only," followed by my initials, and I handed it back to the clerk, thinking perhaps I could give myself an argument, just in case Smith was wrong, and this was not the house in question.

I rode to Alexandria with Jordan the next day. We got along quite well and struck up a lively conversation. As it turned out, Jordan had a love of England, and as I am originally from England, it seemed particularly appropriate that he relayed to me his interest in the poetry of Lord Byron. Jordan was especially fond of Byron and, as it turned out, was something of an expert on his works. Impressively, he had read all Byron's letters and even written a thesis on the basis of them. He recited *Lara* by heart, believing it to be relevant.

He shared with me that he immersed himself in poetry as a way of getting relief from the horror we both saw in our profession—a contrast to our daily exposure to the worst of human nature—and it was a sentiment with which I could truly empathize.

Smith followed us down, a passenger in a prison van. When we arrived, I expressed my hope that we'd come upon the prison truck with its doors wide open and everyone gone. Everyone was amused when I said it was my best hope. Of course, everyone arrived as planned. There was no doubt that Smith had definitely been to the house (or had the house described to him in great detail), for the diagram he had carefully drawn was exact.

Kolman, Jordan, Maio, and I deposed Sullivan in the presence of Smith and a court reporter, and the deposition was later read to the jury. Sullivan testified that she received a call from a man who said he was from Baltimore after she placed the ad in November. According to her recollection, the man came to see the room on a weekday around 5 p.m., but she had no idea what the date was. She confirmed that the man did, in fact, take money from her, telling her he'd be back at 10 p.m. that night, and he never returned. During the deposition, Sullivan noticed Smith with a start and—like a scene from a movie—stood up and pointed, excitedly identifying him as the man who had taken her money.

It couldn't have gone better for us if I'd written the script myself.

Chapter 9: The Trial, Part II

At the start of the trial, all the courtroom personnel were very friendly and convivial; everyone was fresh and interested. We had been together in other stress-filled situations, and there was a bit of a family feel to the courtroom. I tried very hard to maintain that atmosphere whenever I could, throwing in jokes and interacting with familiarity. But, as the days went on, everyone got weary. The starting and recess times varied. Often, Perrott would recess early. He was not a particularly energetic judge and was known to take a headline case and drag it out. However, Perrott soon caught on that I was attempting to create chaos in whatever way I could—it was like trying to stop the inevitable freight train coming down the track. So, he started to get tighter with courtroom personnel.

By the time we were in the third week, he had been pressured by the chief administrative judge to conclude the trial. This was the premier courtroom in the courthouse, and I was stopping the processing of many other cases. So, Judge Perrott started pressing all the participants to expedite their presentations.

Toward the end, he decided we would sit on weekends. He ordered us to report to the courthouse on Saturday mornings at 9 a.m. Just the way he said it gave me a feeling that he would start clamping down tightly on everyone. On one particular Saturday, since court usually started at 10 o'clock on weekdays, I was thrown off my schedule. I turned the corner to walk into the courthouse right at 9 a.m. (I could hear the bells ringing at a nearby church), but I was one minute late entering the courtroom. When I walked in, the jury was in the box, the judge was on the bench, the court reporter was in place, the law clerk and the marshals were in position. No one was saying a word. I breathed a sigh of relief, thinking I was only one minute late, so I could kiss the judge's ass for a minute and make everything right. As soon as I got to the trial table, I apologized profusely for wasting the court's time and for being a minute late. Perrott realized that I had narrowly escaped what he had in store for me. Nevertheless, I got the message to make sure that I moved the case along.

As the trial progressed, I did what I could to prepare for my closing argument, which, in a circumstantial case, is always difficult. There's always a lull after the prosecution has finished its closing arguments. I asked for a recess, so at least I could have some fresh jurors to try to impress. The secret to a good closing argument is to start months before the trial. By halfway through the case, I would have already structured my closing. As the case went on, I would then polish it and give it with no notes. Of course, I would keep some shorthand notes on the trial table in case I choked. But, I realized, it wasn't always bad to choke because jurors want you to be human. If you forget what you were saying or lose your train of thought, it's pretty obvious to everybody, and jurors like you when you admit that you've made mistakes. It makes you human, which makes your argument more compelling, more acceptable.

A lot of people think you win a case in closing argument, but you really don't. And in this case, I sure as hell didn't. There were about 60 high school students on a field trip in the courtroom that day. Their teacher had asked me to talk to the students before the session started, and I happily complied. I joked around with them and let them know I was a real human being, not just some guy in a tie. I had them laughing and listening. Then it turned serious when court was called to order.

From time to time, I would look back at the students, and they seemed interested in what was going on. But, after about 45 minutes into my closing argument, as I was walking back and forth in front of the jury, I turned toward the back of the room

Above Left: Exterior, Clarence M. Mitchell Courthouse on Calvert Street in Baltimore, Maryland, where Smith was tried.

Above Right: Jury box.

Views of the interior lobby, Clarence M. Mitchell Courthouse.

Keating waits for court to resume.

and saw the teacher gesture to the students to leave. Apparently, the school bus was departing, and they could not wait until the end of my speech. All 60 of them started to shuffle out at once. Of course, I stopped—I had no choice.

I glanced over at the judge and he gave me a look that seemed to say, "How do you like that, Keating? Guess they weren't that impressed with your argument." I tried to convey with my eyeballs, "I get it. If could walk out, I would too. And so would you—but we can't and neither can the jurors."

After the interruption, I regained my composure and spoke for another 45 minutes. I was surprised to learn, later, that my closing argument would cover 60 pages of the transcript. Nevertheless, the prosecutors rapidly and succinctly buried me—and more importantly, Smith—in their rebuttal argument.

When the jurors retired to the jury room to consider their verdict, they didn't look over at the defense table, which was about the 55th clue I had that they were going to find Smith guilty

At the end of my closing, I noticed that the armpits on my suit were particularly damp. It had been one of the most difficult closing arguments I'd ever have to make, simply because the evidence was so overwhelming. The only way to argue a circumstantial case is to throw out even more circumstances to obfuscate the ones that compellingly dictate guilt.

It rarely works.

As soon as the jurors retired, a note came out that they were concerned about the evening meal. The judge was more than glad to make arrangements at the House of Welsh, a famous restaurant a couple blocks from the courthouse. Menus were obtained and the marshal took the jurors' orders. He sent out to the restaurant to get their meals and the court personnel decided, at the judge's direction, that we would have our supper actually in the House of Welsh.

We left the courthouse and met at a large table that seated eight of us, which included the prosecutors, the judge, and several clerks. We had just ordered the meal. I was looking forward to biting into a juicy steak when a telephone call came from the courthouse to the restaurant for Judge Perrott. He left the table, returned almost immediately, did not sit down and said, "They have a verdict already. Let's go back and take the verdict." Son of a bitch. I felt like I didn't even get to eat my last meal.

We went back and immediately took the verdict. When the jurors came into the room, again, not one of them looked at me or Smith. The foreman seemed to render the verdict with gusto. Guilty. First-degree murder. They were doing their civic duty and proud to do it. I couldn't blame them.

It was getting dark rapidly when I left the courthouse after the verdict had been rendered. It was usually my practice to go down and commiserate with the defendant in the bullpen. But, in this situation, I didn't feel like holding Smith's hand.

I left the Calvert Street exit of the courthouse and headed to my office a block away. As I turned the corner, I felt something hit my left shoulder and put my hand up and felt around. When I brought my hand back, it was covered with pigeon shit. I looked at it and thought the master of symbolism, Henrik Ibsen, would have loved the message I was being sent: Not your day!

> **C 16   THE SUN, Monday, August 5, 1974**
>
> ## Man guilty of murder in Hampden stabbing
>
> 8/5/74
>
> By GEORGE J. HILTNER
>
> A Criminal Court jury has convicted a 51-year-old man of murder in the first degree in the beating and stabbing of a 65-year-old Hampden woman last November.
>
> "You've convicted an innocent man," James H. Smith, the defendant, told the jurors after they returned the guilty verdict following three hours of deliberation late Friday. The trial lasted three weeks.
>
> Judge James A. Perrott deferred sentencing pending a new-trial motion. Smith faces an automatic life-imprisonment sentence.
>
> Smith was convicted of fatally beating Doris E. Martin, of the 3400 block Chestnut avenue, after answering her newspaper advertisement offering a room to rent.
>
> Mark Kolman, the prosecutor, noted that Smith had used the same method to gain entrance to homes of elderly women on other occasions. Smith has an extensive criminal record, the prosecutor pointed out.
>
> Smith's defense to the killing here was that at the time of the murder, he was in Arlington, Va. "flim-flamming" a 72-year-old woman out of several hundred dollars after answering her room ad.
>
> The Virginia woman, in an affidavit read to the jury, said she could not fix the exact date when Smith took $200 in rent income off her dining room table.
>
> Smith was at liberty on work-release from an Anne Arundel county sentence of 12 years when Mrs. Martin was slain.
>
> He is now serving that term, given him for robbing an Annapolis woman after using the same "m.o." as he identified his modus operandi, to enter her home.
>
> Police testified that Smith admitted the slaying but refused to sign a written statement. Police further told the jurors that blood stains of the victim's blood type were found on Smith's clothing.

1974 article from *The Sun*, upon Smith's conviction.

Chapter 10: The Appeal

After the trial, Smith was not done trying to work around the system. On September 18, 1974, he wrote a letter to Judge Perrott in an apparent, or should I say transparent, attempt to manipulate him. The judge was not swayed, and he sent me a copy of the letter.

> *Dear Judge Perrott:*
>
> *Your honor, I know Mr. Keating my attorney is quite qualified in presenting a case to you on my behalf for a new trial (it is possible that by the time you receive this he has already done so). This might sound idiotic your honor, but I would not now be writing if it hadn't been for a dream I had the other night. In truth I had thought of writing to you right after the trial but veto the thought knowing Mr. Keating would do all he could for me.*
>
> *Prior to the dream the other night I have been living in a constant nightmare (and I still maintain that state). I know if anyone wants to look over my past record no tears would be shed nor would sympathy be voiced. However, I am looking only for the truth to be known. That might sound funny coming from a man who stated on the stand that he lied. Yes, I lied, and because I lied I help wind a web around me, but I am convinced (since the testimony of others) that there are various degrees of lies (such as different degrees in certain*

crimes). *I can assure your honor there were lies told on the stand by (mainly detective Russell and Detective Perkowski and also Mrs. Bishop) who incidentally was to have been a defense witness many months ago, but due to a mystery I hope will be unfold in the future, she became a State witness with a world coach story. The lies told by those three have to be of the highest degree. I firmly believe that the worse crime anyone could commit is to knowingly help convict an innocent person regardless of what the reason behind it is.*

Anyhow Your Honor, the secret truth is that no way I would be capable of committing. It might be hard for you to understand, but do you know I was more concerned about the offense (I more or less had to reveal) that was not known. More concerned because I knew I was guilty of it and had it not been for the unfortunate death of that woman in Hamden, I would not have had to reveal it. I never dreamed it possible to be convicted of something I did not do. That is why I live in this hellish nightmare.

The animal that killed that poor woman is free while I stand convicted to his crime. Actually, I should apologize to animals, because what I heard concerning her death, had to come from something less.

Your honor, I don't know how long you have been a judge or how many cases you have presided over. However, I have heard the name Judge Perrott for many years, therefore it is safe to assume your cases have been many. During the time I was in your court, I found you to be a well-rated man (quoting judge) and that very little (if anything) gets by you unnoticed. "No, I am not conning you—I would not insult your intelligence." Because of your experience, I'm merely asking one thing of you. Please I beg you to personally go over everything you know about this case. I know in my heart that if you do, there will be many question marks that will come to your mind. Certainly a jury can be easily influenced these days, the way vicious crimes are being committed. I am no saint (obviously) but I too despise certain crimes—namely where a life is taken. I have hurt people, but never physically, always it was money wise. I could never have murder on my conscious, because know I could not live with it. There has been something drastically wrong in this whole case from the moment I was questioned about it last December 18.

Many changes of time, after the death have come about. Originally it was the 13th of November, then because it was found that I was locked up that day it was changed to either the 12th or the 13th, then to the 12th alone. Then the times were changed several times to suit the State's case against me. They came to a conclusion that it was somewhere between 6 and 8 p.m. on the 12th. When in fact it was an impossibility for me to be there even at those times. Study the times your honor and you will see. If you go over these things you will see too that something doesn't make sense. As God is my judge, your honor, I am as innocent as you are of killing that woman. There should be many things to warn you for granting a new trial.

But most of all that after going over things, it should be granted because your honor should have doubts and therefore would want no part in sentencing a man when the evidence does not show guilt.

I said at the start that it might sound idiotic in saying I decided to write because of a dream, but I doubt very must if anyone knows the true meaning of dreams (I know I don't) but this one seems likes it was a message to me. Everywhere in the dream—fences, billboards, sidewalks, etc. contained a chalk written, "Write this Judge, Write the Judge." So your honor, I have written and I hope your heart receives a message telling you what is true, "I am innocent." Please help, remove me from this nightmare.

Sincerely,
James Francis Smith

I argued an extensive motion for a new trial on his behalf, making a case that the evidence from the boxes at Buffington's house should have been ruled inadmissible. On December 18,

1974, the judge immediately denied the requested relief and the court imposed life imprisonment.

The Appellate Division of the Office of the Public Defender was a separate and distinct unit from ours. They were, for the most part, more intelligent and much better academic lawyers. At this point, they took over Smith's appeal, which was filed with the Court of Special Appeals (COSA).

Because Smith had not been tried within 120 days (his case had not commenced until the 136th day), the COSA ruled, in February 1976, that, under the Intrastate Detainer Act, the entire trial was a nullity—the conviction was void—and Smith's conviction should be reversed and dismissed with prejudice. In other words, he could not be tried again, all because he had been tried 16 days after the statute said he should have been. Smith and his lawyers did not even have to show any prejudice that occurred to him because of this 16-day delay. The decision was based on strict liability. (You might note that after this conviction was reversed, there was such outrage at this miscarriage of justice that the law was changed as a result. Today, if you commit first degree murder in Maryland and are tried 16 days late, the state might have to apologize, but you will, by no means, be freed.)

As it stood, Smith would not serve any time for the brutal murder of Doris Martin, but he still had to serve the remainder of his 12-year term for the armed robbery of Aspasia Nichols.

As the years went by after Smith's conviction, there was no further publicity or information about him or the case. As far as I was concerned, he was simply over at the penitentiary doing his time. However, on a bright day in July of 1978, I received a call from the Baltimore City Police Department. Carol Buffington had alerted them that Smith was being released early due to good conduct time.

It had always been in the back of my head that Smith had admitted, under oath, to a grand larceny in Virginia, but there were so many murders and serious cases in Maryland and Virginia, no one was concerned about a simple flimflam. Nothing was going to happen unless someone initiated a prosecution, and that just didn't sit well with me.

I had always rationalized representing guilty people with the usual incantations about constitutional protections. Defense of the indefensible was a necessary evil, after all. But I knew that, in reality, I participated because of the challenges and competition I found so stimulating. To salve my conscience, I determined I would not sell my soul or my self-respect to any organized criminal activity. I ensured that I would never be an accomplice or accessory after the fact by never encouraging a client to do something that was not in their own best interest. I also decided I would not represent any client whom I had previously gotten off if they committed a subsequent serious crime. (While this principle kept my conscious clear, it meant I would never make a lot of money off dope dealers or organized criminals.)

But Smith represented an entirely different kind of moral dilemma. I knew he would continue his life of crime and victimize many more helpless, vulnerable women once he was free. My legal obligation to keep quiet about what I knew clashed with my personal concern. I had never met anyone so chilling.

I kept thinking about the two murders he seemed to have committed in Pennsylvania but got away with because of a mediocre alibi. I replayed how he had brutalized and sodomized his victim in Annapolis. I couldn't shake the thought that Doris Martin died a brutal death because this maniac had been set free on work release. Madness! The system was broken.

I had never liked brutal cowards ... ever, yet I had—as the result of my conscientious good lawyering and maneuvering—played the speedy trial scenario well and gotten one acquitted. We beat first degree murder because of a technicality. One hundred thirty-seven days to the start of the trial was just 16 days too late, and I had papered the courthouse with necessary motions, never truly believing Smith would be given his freedom after a full trial showing his guilt and absolutely dangerous nature.

His release date was imminent and no one was paying attention. I realized it was up to me. After much reflection about loyalty to Smith, the system, the rule of law, the defense function and sensibilities, I decided not to equivocate. Fuck him! I was certain Smith should be prevented at all costs from having the chance to devastate the community again. I would help justice prevail and help keep Smith locked up for as long as possible. I just had to figure out how to do it secretly, and—as fate may have it—the opportunity presented itself quite nicely.

Soon after, I found myself relaxing one evening with a good friend of mine, Sam Brave, who was in the Prosecutor's Office. I started ruminating about the case and told him that I thought his office was failing—that a killer would soon be released from the penitentiary and that, no doubt, he would rip off a whole bunch of vulnerable people and likely kill and sexually assault others again. In my mind, I told him, there really was no question that this was going to happen, and if I were still in the Prosecutor's Office, I would get any judge I could to prosecute the recidivist psychopath for the grand larceny he admitted to under oath.

I prevailed on Brave to follow through. He promptly contacted Kolman and Jordan (who had moved on to the U.S. Attorney's Office at that point) and wrote a succinct 12-page summary of Smith's situation. Brave asked the authorities in Virginia to undertake extradition proceedings, so Smith could be transferred there to be prosecuted for the grand larceny he admitted to during the Martin trial.

A few months went by and Brave informed me that, in fact, the attorney general in Virginia had decided to extradite Smith, and the paperwork was being processed. Several more months passed before Smith was transferred to Virginia—just a month before he was going to be released on the armed robbery case in Maryland.

Once Smith was in Virginia, he was prosecuted and had no choice but to plead guilty—he had admitted to the crime under oath. He received what I thought to be an excessively appropriate sentence of 10 years for grand larceny.

But, Smith would, once again, work his way around justice. He was released from that sentence after less than one year—for supplying information on another inmate who confessed a murder to him.

Room for Rent

E SUN
Friday, February 20, 1976

Murder verdict nullified

Appeals court finds speedy trial denied

By ROBERT P. WADE
Annapolis Bureau of The Sun

Annapolis—The 1974 murder conviction of a state prison inmate was thrown out yesterday by the Court of Special Appeals, along with charges that he murdered a 65-year-old Hampden woman.

The court ruled that the inmate had been denied a speedy trial. The man was brought to trial July 8, 1974, just 16 days after a statutory 120-day limit ran out.

James Francis Smith was charged with stabbing and beating to death Doris E. Martin, who had lived by herself in the 3400 block Chestnut avenue.

Prosecutors alleged during the trial that Smith had gone to the woman's house in response to a room-for-rent newspaper advertisement.

Smith was on a work-release program from the prison camp in Jessup at the time.

The 53-year-old admitted con artist denied murdering the woman and as an alibi presented evidence that he was in Alexandria, Va., at the time of her murder "flim-flamming" another woman.

During testimony, he admitted that answering room-for-rent ads was part of his confidence operation.

A jury convicted Smith in August, 1974, and he was sentenced to life in prison for first-degree murder. He had previously been serving a 12-year term for robbing an Annapolis woman.

But the state's case had been ruined before it even came to trial, though prosecutors apparently did not realize it at the time.

The case ran afoul of a Maryland statute called the "Intrastate Detainer Act," which gives an inmate charged with a crime while he is serving

See MARTIN, C2, Col. 1

Court voids murder verdict, cites trial delay

MARTIN, from C1

time an opportunity to ask for prompt disposition of the charges.

When a prisoner makes such a request, the state has 120 days to bring him to trial, unless "for good cause shown in court" a judge grants any "necessary or reasonable continuance."

Smith was informed, according to court records, of the charges facing him February 6, 1974.

His request for a speedy trial was received in Baltimore Criminal Court February 19 and by Milton B. Allen, who was state's attorney at the time, and Judge Dulany Foster, who was then chief judge of the Supreme Bench, February 22.

In the opinion of the special appeals court, the 120 days began running at that time.

Smith was brought before Judge Paul Dorf April 11, 1974, for his arraignment. His trial was scheduled for April 22, but Judge Dorf ordered the man sent to Clifton T. Perkins State Hospital for a psychiatric examination.

The judge requested a report from the hospital within 60 days, or by July 11 at the latest.

But Smith, who had protested that he was sane and that he did not want to go to Perkins, remained at the Maryland Penitentiary from April 11 to June 10 before he was finally sent to the hospital.

The appeals court blamed that delay on "bureaucratic foul-ups," the very sort of mixups the detainer law is supposed to protect inmates against.

"When he finally got to Perkins," the opinion said, "the complete evaluation was finished within 17 days.

"Nor may we excuse the failure of the state, as the June 22 deadline was approaching, to make every effort to expedite the case and bring the appellant to trial within the prescribed time or to go into open court and seek a necessary continuance at that time."

Even with the reversal, Smith will remain in prison, at least for the time being.

Smith is now an inmate at the Maryland Correctional Institution in Hagerstown, and the time he has left to serve on the previous charge could keep him locked up until spring of 1979, according to a prison spokesman, unless he is paroled before then.

Mr. Allen, newly appointed as a judge in Baltimore, said he could not recall the specific details of the case.

But he remarked that problems in moving inmates between prisons and other institutions or even getting them from the jail to the courthouse was a headache in the past and remains so.

1976 article from the Annapolis Bureau of *The Sun*, upon the overturning of Smith's conviction.

A chilling Christmas card received by the Office of the Public Defender in 1976, handwritten and illustrated by Smith after his conviction was overturned but while he was still incarcerated for his crime against Nichols.

Smith's greeting reads:

> There are many things i would like to say ...
> There are some things i will never say ...
> But let me say this ...
> "Merry Christmas!!"
>
> James F. Smith

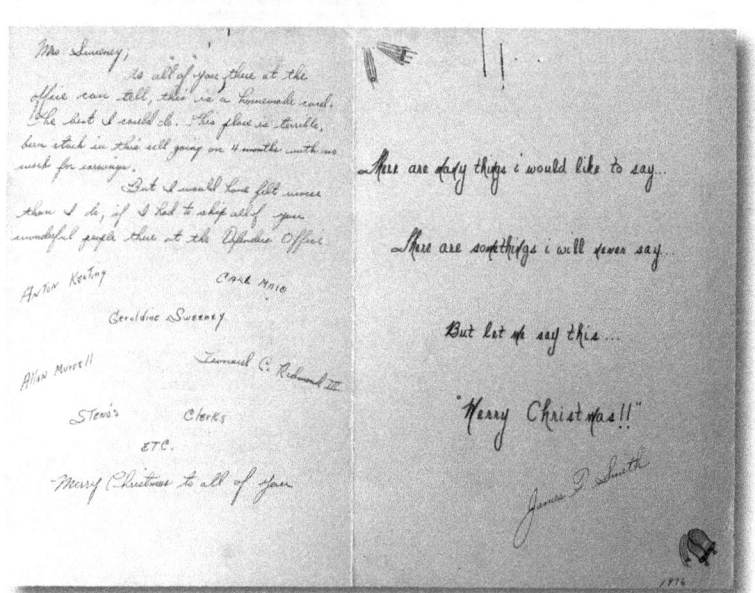

Smith's personal note to the Office of the Public Defender reads:

Mrs. Sweeney;
    As all of you there at the office can tell, this is a homemade card. The best I could do. This place is terrible, been stuck in this cell going on 4 months with no work for earnings.
    But I would have felt worse than I do, if I had to skip all of you wonderful people there at the Defenders Office.

Chapter 11:
Lady Justice Weighs In

Once again, some time passed before I thought of Smith. When I finally did check up on him, I was startled to find that he was no longer in prison in Virginia. I set about finding out where he was and discovered that he had made his way to California, where he continued to behave like the recidivist sociopath that he was.

I found a Sacramento Superior Court document that painted a very clear picture of Smith's criminal life, beginning well before I met him. The document detailed a multitude of instances where he had run his traditional flimflam scheme and several instances where he became extremely violent. Of note was a description of a couple of offenses on a report received from the City of Pittsburgh, Pennsylvania. The evidence that Smith was the perpetrator was overwhelming, but it was also circumstantial, and he had been able to evade prosecution for the charges.

> *... [T]he defendant was arrested on March 24, 1958, for assault and battery with intent to ravish. At that time, the victim of the offense, the owner of a boarding house in which the defendant was a boarder, went to the defendant's room after which he offered her a hot dog and a glass of milk. Subsequently, both she and the defendant went to her room where she sat upon her bed. The defendant sat beside her and subsequently placed his arm around her and began to pull up her dress. The victim stated, "don't touch me" after which*

the defendant stated to her, "don't start hollering or I'll hurt you." The defendant then placed his hand over her mouth and pushed her out of the room. The victim was able to escape from the defendant's grasp and run from her residence after which she contacted the Pittsburgh Police Department which resulted in the defendant's arrest. The charge of assault and battery with intent to ravish was later dismissed by the Allegheny County Court.

According to a memo addressed to Chief John F. Stack, the Allegheny County Detective Bureau, in Pittsburgh, Pennsylvania, from a Captain Joseph J. Start, of the Homicide Division, dated February 7, 1974, the defendant was listed as a suspect in a murder of a 72 years old adult female, which occurred on November 29, 1962. According to that memo ... the victim of the homicide was found lying face down, completely submerged in a bathtub, which was three-quarters filled with water. Officers observed extensive bruises to the victim's hands and arms, and rope marks on the victim's wrist. After the crime scene was worked, it was concluded that the initial attack took place in the victim's bedroom closet. Blood stains were evident on the walls of that closet and some were observed on the floor. Further, the drapery cords to the victim's bedroom draperies had been cut and were subsequently found, soaked with water, in the victim's garbage. During the course of their investigations, it was learned that the victim had made arrangements to rent the guest room in her residence and had in fact made an appointment to show the guest room to an unknown man that afternoon.

Officers interviewed the victim's daughter who informed officers that her mother had always rented a room to men and had done so for approximately the past fifteen years since her father's death. She stated that three days prior to her mother's death, her mother had received a call from a man inquiring about the room for rent. The man identified himself as Danny Foster and stated that he was the head of a surveying crew that would be working in the area and that he would like a nice room in a good home. Further, she stated that her mother had *informed her that "Mr. Foster was being transferred to the Pittsburgh area from Connecticut and that he had spoke of losing his wife and son in an airplane crash." "Mr. Foster" had made an appointment to see the room on November 27, 1962, however, he called on that date to cancel the appointment giving the reason that his equipment had not as yet arrived in town and that he was concerned about it. After making the above statement, concluding their conversation, he again called a few minutes later and advised that he would be out at 3:00 or 3:30 p.m. to see the room.*

At approximately 3:00 p.m. on that date, the victim's daughter received a phone call from the victim at which time the victim informed her that she had just received a call from the "Railway Express Company" in Pittsburgh and that a man allegedly representing that company had asked to speak to "Danny Foster." The victim informed the caller that "Mr. Foster" had not as yet arrived and thus the caller asked if upon his arrival, she would inform him that all of his tools were at the Pittsburgh Railway Station in the Pennsylvania Station in Pittsburgh. Additionally, the caller had equipment and that "Mr. Foster" had to pick up these items before 6:00 in the evening or they would be sent back to Connecticut. She indicated that during the course of this conversation with her mother, her mother stated, "There's someone coming up the walk now. I'll call you back."

Subsequently, the victim's daughter stated that she had attempted to call her mother approximately one hour later but the line was busy. She tried again later and when she received no answer to her call, she and her husband went to her mother's address where they subsequently discovered her body in the bathtub of the residence.

Neighbors of the decedent were interviewed and ... officers received a description of a white male adult who was seen in the neighborhood on the afternoon of the victim's death. He was described as being approximately 5'9" tall, 150 to 160 pounds, very neat in appearance, with reddish brown hair, parted on the left side of his head.

In view of the description on given by the decedent's neighbors, and the "Modus Operandi" as related by the decedent's daughter, the defendant, James Francis Smith, was considered a possible suspect. According to the Chief of Police of the Bellevue Police Department, the defendant had been previously positively identified in two other similar crimes but had not been tried on those crimes as the ladies involved were quite elderly. In both of the above two cases, the defendant had come to the elderly women's home in regard to an advertisement they had placed in the paper for a room to rent. Upon arrival at the homes, the defendant asked to use the toilet facilities and upon exiting the bedroom, he immediately grabbed the ladies, threw them on the floor, while punching and slapping them. He then helped them up onto a bed within the residence, tied their hands with a cord and bound their ankles. He would then torment the victims by holding his hand over their mouths and pinching their nostrils together, so they could not breathe. Each of the victims indicated to the police officers that prior to the defendant's having arrived in their residence and while making arrangements to see their rooms for rent, he had indicated that both his wife and son had been killed in an airplane crash.

Having accumulated the above information, the defendant was taken into custody for questioning regarding the above mentioned homicide. He was placed in a lineup and although several of the decedent's neighbors indicated that he looked like the individual they had seen in the neighborhood, none of them could positively identify him. The defendant gave police officers an alibi for the time established to have been the decedent's time of death, but when police officers broke the defendant's story, the defendant refused to discuss the case any further. The defendant retained a lawyer and was granted his release on a Writ of Habeas Corpus.

Two other incidents were detailed in that same Pittsburgh report. They were the first attacks I was aware of that didn't involve Smith's traditional con. The first detailed a violent attack that occurred on December 16, 1979. The victim was a 60-year-old woman.

According to the victim, she had met the defendant, as James Clark approximately two weeks prior at the Casino Bar in North Sacramento. Since that time, the defendant had called her on several occasions asking her for a date.

On December 16, 1979, she invited the defendant over to her duplex for dinner. The defendant arrived approximately 5:00 p.m., after which she and the defendant sat at the dining room table and conversed for approximately a two-hour period of time. She indicated upon initially meeting the defendant, he had informed her that his wife had died approximately eight years ago in a plane crash but that on this evening, he had informed her that he had lied and that in actuality his wife was 76 years of age and was confined to a wheelchair. The defendant informed her that they were going to dissolve their marriage at which time she informed him that she did not go out with married men.

... [T]he defendant got up from his chair and walked to where she was seated. He grabbed her by the hands and pulled her from the chair to her feet. He then tied her hands behind her back with a dog leash and stated, "shut up, and get in there," pushing her in the direction of the master bedroom. Once in the bedroom, he removed her clothing and forced her to lie face down on the bed .... Subsequently, he took a pair of her panties and instructed her to open her mouth. When she refused, the defendant took a knife and placed it at her neck. As a result, the victim opened her mouth and the defendant took the panties he was holding and shoved them into her mouth. At this point, the defendant left her bedroom after covering her with a blanket. After an unknown time, the defendant re-entered her bedroom, pulled the blanket off her and replaced the panties, which she had managed to

remove from her mouth, back into her mouth. At this time, the defendant stated, "I have a big nigger friend that's coming to screw you." He checked the victim's hands and stated that he would have to loosen the ties. He removed the dog leash which bound her hands and retied her hands using a pair of her pantyhose.

Later in the evening, the victim heard water running. Subsequently, the defendant entered her room, helped her up from the bed and forced her to enter one of the two bathrooms in her residence. Upon entering the bathroom, the victim noticed that the bathtub was almost completely filled up. At this time, the defendant forced the victim to get into the bathtub. Although the victim was crying and pleading with the defendant to stop tormenting her, the defendant ignored her and forced her to remain within the bathtub for an undetermined length of time. Subsequently, after the water in the bathtub became "almost cold," the defendant instructed her to get out. The defendant quickly patted her with a towel and instructed her to get back into bed. When she did so, the defendant again covered her with blankets.

Toward the early morning hours of December 17, 1979, the defendant, according to the victim, became "remorseful." She indicated that the defendant stated, "I don't know why I did this. I was a real animal. I know you are a respectable person." At approximately 7:00 a.m., the defendant untied the victim, went into the living room of her residence and telephoned for a cab. He made a second call to the cab company and finally left the residence at approximately 8:00 a.m.

The second attack that was described was, once again, violent and not related to Smith's usual room-for-rent scheme. The victim was his youngest yet, a 54-year-old woman.

On [September 10, 1980, the victim] had gone to the Carousel Lounge ... While there she danced and conversed with the defendant, who she knew as Jim Clark, and who had been introduced to her approximately one week earlier.

During the course of the evening, the defendant offered to give her a ride home as she was tired and her friend was not as yet ready to go home.

She accepted the defendant's offer and they left the lounge. While in route to what the victim believed was her residence, the defendant insisted that they stop at the Peppermill Restaurant. While there, the defendant informed the victim that he had an expensive gift to give her as she reminded him of his former wife who had been killed in a plane crash. The defendant insisted that they go to his residence to get the gift as it was his intention to leave early the next day for the State of Nevada ... Upon arrival, she asked to use the bathroom. When she exited the bathroom, the defendant was holding a knife, grabbed the victim by her throat and stated, "Bitch, I'm going to rape you, and then I'm going to kill you." She was able to escape from his grasp and ran to the front door. However, while she was in the bathroom, the defendant had secured the front door with three separate locks. She ran to the back door of the residence. That door had three locks, all of which were engaged. The defendant again approached her, placing one hand at her throat while holding a knife in his other hand. The defendant stated, "Get in the bedroom." The victim followed the defendant's instructions. Once in the bathroom, she kicked the defendant in the groin with her knee, threw him on the bed, and bit his ear. She grabbed the knife that the defendant was holding, and while sitting on top of him, stabbed him on the back of his head. She stabbed him numerous times, during the course of which the blade to the knife broke off at the handle.

Following the break of the knife, she told Smith that if he would just allow her to leave, she would allow him to get up off the bed. Before she allowed him to get up the victim reached into her purse and retrieved a "rat-tail" comb which had a long pointed handle. As soon as she allowed him to get up off the bed, he immediately ran to the front door and picked up a metal rod and said viciously "You see, I can still kill you." She ran to the back door of the residence where she had earlier seen a screwdriver which was holding one of the locks to that door in place. She removed the screwdriver from the lock and held it as a means of self-protection.

The defendant held her captive for a couple of hours, not allowing her to leave, during which time she pleaded with him to allow her to go. He opened the front door of his residence allowing the victim to exit and instructed her to get into his vehicle which she did. As he backed his vehicle out of the driveway she escaped through the passenger's door of the vehicle. She ran from the scene to seek help. It was a short time later that the victim contacted the Sacramento Police Department while taking refuge in a residence near that of the defendant's.

On September 23, 1980, after viewing the photographs, the victim pointed to the photograph of Smith and said, "Number two—My God, it's him, it's him." She informed the police officers that she "Knew the suspect was going to get her now and that if she ended up dead the police will know that who killed her."

Later, Smith would eventually admit to all of these charges; however, he denied any assault with the intent to commit rape but offered no alternate explanation as to his behavior with that victim.

The Sacramento Police Department had Smith on its radar for a while, but, unsurprisingly they were having a hard time charging him with anything that would stick. But, October 22, 1980, would prove to be a fateful day for Smith.

Officer Souza received a phone call from Sergeant Shaw, requesting assistance contacting a woman named Lorrain Kirby to gather information about a possible fraud scheme that was in the process of occurring. The police report from that incident said:

> Miss Kirby ... [informed them] that she had been in contact with a friend of hers, another victim who had lost money to a male who had contacted her regarding a room to rent. On

this date, October 22, 1980, she had received a telephone call from a male subject regarding a room she had listed in the newspaper for rent and the circumstances of the call sounded similar to that of her friend as indicated above.

Miss Kirby had received a call at 12:45 p.m., regarding her advertised room. The caller said that one of his construction workers was in route to Sacramento and upon arrival would need a place to stay. At approximately 1:15 p.m. a male subject who identified himself as "Frank" contacted her by phone and stated that his boss had called earlier regarding a room arrangement and that he needed her name and address so that he could have his belongings shipped to the residence. Miss Kirby gave the caller, "Frank," a fictitious name and address. Approximately thirty minutes later, "Frank called again and stated that he was at the Greyhound Bus Depot and while at that location someone had stolen his wallet which he had left in a phone booth at the depot. He then asked Miss Kirby to request $400.00 for him of anyone who might call to her residence for him. At approximately 3:10 p.m. a caller contacted Miss Kirby and requested to speak to "Frank." Miss Kirby informed the caller that Frank was not as yet at the address, however, he, "Frank," had requested that $400.00 to be sent to him at her address. The caller stated that the banks were all closed but that he would send the money on the following date, October 23, 1980.

At approximately 3:30 p.m., on a telephone call that was taped by police officers, "Frank" called Miss Kirby and informed her that he was attempting to obtain money in downtown Sacramento to pay for surveying equipment that was scheduled to arrive in town and he would call back later in the day.

At 4:05 p.m. "Frank" again called, this conversation was again taped by police officers, informing Miss Kirby that he was unable to obtain any money. As a result, Miss Kirby told "Frank" that she would loan him $220.00. Miss Kirby agreed to meet with "Frank" at the Greyhound Bus Depot at 7:00 p.m. Miss Kirby was given ten twenty-dollar bills, whose serial *numbers had been recorded, in an envelope by Sacramento Police Officers.*

At 7:00 p.m., Miss Kirby met with "Frank" at the corner of 7th and L Streets in downtown Sacramento. They then went inside a "Burger King" restaurant at that location. After being seated in the restaurant, and following a brief conversation, Miss Kirby passed to "Frank" the white envelope containing the money given to her by police officers. Shortly thereafter, Miss Kirby excused herself to go to the women's restroom and following her exit, "Frank" was approached by police officers and taken into custody. "Frank," was in fact, the defendant, James Francis Smith.

On January 7, 1981, Smith was finally arrested by officers of the Sacramento Sheriff's Department and charged with several crimes, including assault with a deadly weapon and false imprisonment. According to the District Attorney's Office, these charges were dropped as the victim of the offense did not want to go through the ordeal entailed in prosecuting the defendant. Nevertheless, they had enough evidence against Smith that he pleaded guilty to assault with intent to commit rape, use of a weapon, and grand theft.

He was sentenced to seven years and eight months. While serving this sentence, Smith developed leukemia. In 1988, just a few months shy of his release, he died in prison.

Finally, a sentence he couldn't escape.

Mug shot of Smith from May 1970, when he was booked for the violent crime against Aspasia Nichols in Annapolis, Maryland.

Epilogue

The verdict had been returned, and I felt a welcome sense of relief that the case had finally concluded. Nevertheless, I tossed and turned for two or three hours before I was finally able to sleep that night. I had no commitments for the following day, but when I awoke, I was initially panicked by the fact that it was 9:30, and I thought I would be late for court.

When the panic subsided, I wandered around my bedroom not knowing where to go first. I was not quite ready to put the case and the intriguing facts and personalities to rest, so I decided to write some witty poem about the trial and send it to the prosecutors and the judge. I wondered if the case might lend itself to some humor, since I seemed to be able to find humor anywhere, and a camaraderie and mutual respect had developed between the prosecutors, the judge, and myself—as unlikely as that may seem.

After drinking a cup of coffee, I selected an anthology of poetry to give me some ideas. I then recalled the conversation I had with Gary Jordan on the way back from Alexandria, where he and I had spent a pleasant hour discussing his love of Byron.

I flipped through the anthology of English literature to the section on Lord Byron until I landed on *Lara*. It then occurred to me that, perhaps, I could use a Byronic style, plugging in relevant words that would be recognizable as the poet's signature form.

However, as I proceeded from line to line, I discovered that—with just a few very minor word changes—an excerpt from

Byron's poem seemed to fit James Francis Smith to an uncanny degree. I felt the similarities to be so bizarre, and the concepts so dynamic, that I decided to let the poem remain—for the most part—unchanged by my weak efforts.

The emotions contained in the poem were so strong that I decided against any attempts at comedy. It took three hours before I could sweep my fascination with the poem aside. I had misgivings about the possibility of ennobling Smith by associating him with such beauty and brilliance contained in Lord Byron's poetry. However, ambivalent as I was, the poem did give me some needed closure, and *Lara* won me over.

My secretary, accustomed to peculiar requests, gladly typed the hundred odd lines and, as my last official act before vacation, I hand delivered copies to the prosecutors and judge, wondering if they would appreciate it as much as I had.

Excerpt from *Lara* by Lord Byron

XVII.

In him inexplicably mix'd appeared
Much to be loved and hated, sought and feared;
Opinion varying o'er his hidden lot,
In praise or railing ne'er his name forgot;
His silence formed a theme for others' prate —
They guess'd — they gazed — they fain would know his fate.
What had he been? what was he, thus unknown,
Who walked their world, his lineage only known?
A hater of his kind? yet some would say,
With them he could seem gay amidst the gay;
But own'd, that smile, if oft observed and near,
Waned in its mirth and withered to a sneer;
That smile might reach his lip, but passed not by,
None e'er could trace its laughter to his eye:
Yet there was softness too in his regard,
At times, a heart as not by nature hard,
But once perceiv'd, his spirit seem'd to chide
Such weakness as unworthy of its pride,
And steel'd itself, as scorning to redeem
One doubt from others' half withheld esteem;
In self-inflicted penance of a breast
Which tenderness might once have wrung from rest;
In vigilance of grief that would compel
The soul to hate for having lov'd too well.

XVIII.

There was in him a vital scorn of all:
As if the worst had fall'n which could befall,
He stood a stranger in this breathing world,
An erring spirit from another hurled;
A thing of dark imaginings, that shaped
By choice the perils he by chance escaped;
But 'scaped in vain, for in their memory yet
His mind would half exult and half regret:
With more capacity for love than earth
Bestows on most of mortal mould and birth,
His early dreams of good outstripp'd the truth,
And troubled manhood followed baffled youth;
With thought of years in phantom chase misspent,
And wasted powers for better purpose lent;
And fiery passions that had poured their wrath
In hurried desolation o'er his path,
And left the better feelings all at strife
In wild reflection o'er his stormy life;
But haughty still and loath himself to blame,
He called on Nature's self to share the shame,
And charged all faults upon the fleshly form
She gave to clog the soul, and feast the worm;
Till he at last confounded good and ill,
And half mistook for fate the acts of will:
Too high for common selfishness, he could
At times resign his own for others' good,
But not in pity, not because he ought,
But in some strange perversity of thought,
That swayed him onward with a secret pride
To do what few or none would do beside;
And this same impulse would in tempting time
Mislead his spirit equally to crime;
So much he soared beyond, or sunk beneath,
The men with whom he felt condemned to breathe,
And longed by good or ill to separate
Himself from all who shared his mortal state;
His mind abhorring this had fixed her throne

Far from the world, in regions of her own;
Thus coldly passing all that passed below,
His blood in temperate seeming now would flow:
Ah! happier if it ne'er with guilt had glowed,
But ever in that icy smoothness flowed!
'Tis true, with other men their path he walked,
And like the rest in seeming did and talked,
Nor outraged Reason's rules by flaw nor start,
His madness was not of the head, but heart;
And rarely wandered in his speech, or drew
His thoughts so forth as to offend the view.

XIX.

With all that chilling mystery of mien,
And seeming gladness to remain unseen,
He had (if 'twere not nature's boon) an art
Of fixing memory on another's heart:
It was not love perchance — nor hate — nor aught
That words can image to express the thought;
But they who saw him did not see in vain,
And once beheld, would ask of him again:
And those to whom he spake remembered well,
And on the words, however light, would dwell:
None knew, nor how, nor why, but he entwined
Himself perforce around the hearer's mind;
There he was stamp'd, in liking, or in hate,
If greeted once; however brief the date
That friendship, pity, or aversion knew,
Still there within the inmost thought he grew.
You could not penetrate his soul, but found,
Despite your wonder, to your own he wound;
His presence haunted still; and from the breast
He forced an all unwilling interest;
Vain was the struggle in that mental net,
His spirit seem'd to dare you to forget![7]

---

7. Byron, George Gordon Byron, Baron, 1788-1824. Lord Byron. New York: Garland Pub., 1985.

Appendix A: Chronology

1922

April 22
James "Jimmie" Francis Smith is born in Pennsylvania. He has a troubled childhood with an unstable family life and becomes an extremely violent career criminal and con man.

1964

May 25
Smith is sentenced to 10 years in Baltimore City for false pretenses.

1969

March 17
Smith is paroled for 1964 false pretenses charge.

August
Smith meets Carole Buffington.

September 25
Smith robs several women in Annapolis, Maryland.

1970

May 6
Smith is sentenced to 12 years in the Maryland State Penitentiary for armed robbery of an Annapolis, Maryland woman. Parole is revoked from 1964 false pretenses charge, and Smith must serve the rest of that sentence before beginning this one.

December
Smith is transferred to minimum security prison in Hagerstown, Maryland, and learns to be a cook.

1972

February 2
Smith ends sentence for 1964 false pretenses charge and begins 12-year sentence for September 1969 armed robbery.

July 3
Smith is placed on work release and is employed by Sheraton Motor Inn in Hagerstown, Maryland.

1973

August
Smith is denied parole but recommended for work release program.

September
Smith is transferred to the Maryland Correctional Training Center where he works as a cook.

October
Smith is approached by Andretti and offered a "Christmas commutation." Smith is transferred to the Jessup Correctional Camp Center.

November 6
Smith is placed on work release and signs form to work 4 p.m. to midnight at The Emerson Restaurant in Baltimore City.

November 7
Smith arrives at the Emerson Restaurant in Baltimore City and discovers the position has been rejected by the work release authorities because it was not a permanent position.

November 8–9, 12
Smith is inadvertently left on work release transportation list and leaves prison each day. He says he was job hunting.

November 11
Doris Martin advertises a room for rent in *The Sunday Sun*.

November 12
Martin calls her neighbors and informs them that she found a renter for the room. Smith goes to meet Martin.

November 13
Martin is found dead inside her home. Smith is transferred to the Maryland House of Correction after it is discovered that he violated the rules of the work release program.

December 11
Detectives Russell and Perkowski interview Carol Buffington and take Smith's possessions into police custody.

December 18
Smith is brought to the Homicide Office and questioned by Detectives Russell and Perkowski.

1974

January 1
Alan H. Murrell leaves a note for Anton Keating that assigns him to defend Smith.

January 16
Smith is put in a police lineup, but witnesses Locke and Laegel fail to identify him.

January 25
Smith is indicted in the Criminal Court of Baltimore City and charged with murder in the first degree.

January 28
Keating is officially assigned to Smith's case.

January 31
Keating sends request for information to Public Defense Office investigators.

February 19
Keating and Kathy Koshell visit Smith in prison for the first time.

March 18
Keating writes to Smith trying to clarify facts, hoping to delay trial to avoid a particular judge to maximize the chance of success. Arraignment is scheduled for April 11, 1974.

April 1
Carol Buffington tells Keating of Smith's claim that he was in Virginia, scamming another person on the night of the murder. Keating visits Smith again urging him to plead insanity. He tells Smith of the need to postpone the trial to improve his chances of not being executed.

April 11
Smith is arraigned. Keating attempts to file a plea of not guilty by reason of insanity against Smith's desires and Judge Dorf refuses to accept plea. A plea of not guilty is entered.

April 15
Judge Dorf sends Keating a letter from Smith asking for removal of Keating as his attorney. Judge Dorf tells Smith later in court that "Mr. Keating is going to be your attorney."

June 10
Smith is admitted to the Perkins Hospital for a psychiatric evaluation.

July 8
The trial begins before Judge James Perrott. During the trial, Smith confesses to a crime in Alexandria, Virginia, writes letter diagramming Sullivan's residence and gives it to the judge, sealed in an envelope.

August 2
Smith is convicted of murdering Martin.

December 18
Motion for a new trial denied. Smith is sentenced to life in prison, to be served consecutively with his sentence for his 1969 armed robbery conviction in Annapolis, Maryland.

<u>1976</u>

February
Smith's conviction is overturned because of the trial delay and a violation of Smith's right to a speedy trial. Smith remains in prison to finish out his previous armed robbery sentence.

1978

July
Buffington alerts the Baltimore Police Department office by telephone that Smith is due for release from his 12-year armed robbery sentence shortly; he is released early as a result of good conduct time.

August
Brave and Perkowski meet with Alexandria, Virginia, prosecutors and alert them to Smith's crime against Virginia Sullivan.

September
The Virginia Commonwealth's Attorney's Office formally starts prosecution against Smith for Sullivan crime.

1979

January
Smith is released from 12-year armed robbery sentence.

April
Smith is convicted of grand larceny for the Sullivan crime in Virginia and is sentenced to 6 years. He is quickly released from sentence for supplying information on another inmate who confessed a murder to him. He travels to California and flimflams/cons other victims.

1980

September
Smith attempts to rape and rob a 54-year-old victim who successfully fights back.

1981

April 2
Smith is sentenced to 7 years and 8 months for attempted murder.

1988

Months from release, Smith dies in prison of leukemia.

APPENDIX B:
LETTER RE CRIMINAL CHARGES AGAINST SMITH IN VIRGINIA

(The State's Attorney's Office of Baltimore City followed up with this letter to authorities in Virginia regarding instituting criminal charges against Smith.[8])

September 19, 1978

TO: Rawles Jones, Esq.
RE: James Francis Smith

Dear Mr. Jones:

This is by way of a formal follow-up to our recent meeting in Alexandria, Virginia in which we discussed the possibility of instituting criminal proceedings against the above-named individual.

I. BACKGROUND

As you will recall, James Francis Smith, was convicted in Baltimore City in 1974 for murder in the 1st degree for the 1973 slaying of Doris Martin. The victim, Doris Martin, died as a result of multiple stab wounds and a crushed skull. Although it could not be introduced at his trial, Smith is known to have committed at least one other homicide and is suspected to have committed several other unsolved homicides, all involving a similar mode of operation. Smith's conviction was reversed by the Court of Special Appeals of Maryland in February 1976 for the reason that the State failed to comply with the Intra-State Detainer Act which provides that unless there be good cause shown, an individual MUST be brought to trial within 120 days.

Smith committed the Doris Martin murder on November 12, 1973 while on work-release from a 1969 conviction for armed robbery for which he was sentenced to a term of 12 years. That sentence is due to expire on or about December 1, 1978 at which time he will become a free man.

During the course of his trial here in Baltimore for the 1973 murder of Doris Martin, Smith testified under oath in his own "Alibi" defense. He stated in substance that he could not have killed Mrs. Martin on November 12, 1973 because on that date he was in Alexandria, Virginia committing the crime of larceny over $100.00 upon a Virginia Sullivan who had placed an ad in the November 9, 1973 edition of *The Washington Post* advertising a room for rent. While he was unsure of Mrs. Sullivan's address, he testified that she lived a few blocks away from a large Masonic Temple. Mrs. Virginia Sullivan, 2400 King Street, was deposed under oath, subject to cross-examination and she was able to recall vividly that on or about November 12, 1973, (she was not certain of the exact date) the defendant did answer her Washington Post room advertisement and did remove $200.00 from her purse lying on the kitchen table and fled.

As evidence in support of the above facts, the following documentation is supplied herewith:

1. <u>Exhibit No. 1</u> (transcript of testimony of James Francis Smith containing full judicial confession of the above larceny)

> T.25: Reference to the fat that Smith was "still short $350.00" of the $800.00 he needed to pay an individual named Andretti to effectuate an early release.

T.28 through 51: Full narrative of trip by bus from Baltimore, Maryland to Alexandria, Virginia in which he admits stealing $350.00 or $360.00 from Virginia Sullivan who lived near a Masonic Temple.

Admits writing sometime in March 1974 to his girlfriend, Carole Buffington, stating to her that he is innocent of the Doris Martin slaying because he was elsewhere (Alexandria, Va.) committing another crime. See also Exhibit No. 6 which is the letter he refers to. Letter contains full written confession in Smith's own handwriting.

Introduction into evidence of Washington Post newspaper dated November 9, 1973 advertising rooms for rent which includes add placed by Virginia Sullivan.

"I was in Virginia, I absconded some money, I broke the law."

Carole Buffington, Exhibit No. 6 requesting her to obtain copy of Washington Post November 9, 1973 in order to verify his alibi.

Admits confession to Alexandria, Va. Crime to Corporal William George, Maryland State Police.

Testimony regarding change of clothes Smith brought with him to Baltimore, Maryland in order to look more presentable for his meeting with Virginia Sullivan.

Admits wearing sport coat in Alexandria, Virginia.

Repeat of confession.

Repeat of confession.

Repeat of admission made to Corporal George.
Mrs. Sullivan relates how she placed an ad in *The Washington Post* sometime in November or December 1973 (T.437); that her telephone # is 836-2126 corresponding to the phone # listed in the ad dated November 9, 1973 (T.438); that she lives 3 blocks from a Masonic Temple (T.438); she identifies as Smith came to her house at approximately 5 P.M. (T.442); that Smith was shown a room (T.443); that while her back was turned for a moment, Smith took $200.00 from her kitchen counter (T.453); that she never reported the incident to the police because she felt she could not provide police with any information (T.447).

Sergeant George testifies that he interviewed Smith on July 7, 1974 (T.463) at which time Smith admitted going to Washington, D.C. on November 12, 1973 by Trailways Bus and from there to Alexandria, Virginia by taxi-cab to a woman's house near a Masonic Temple where he stole $360.00 from a woman who had placed an ad in *The Washington Post* newspaper from a room for rent.

(Letter from *Washington Post* dated July 16, 1974 confirming that Mrs. Virginia Sullivan did place an ad in the classified section on November 9, 1973).

---

8. This letter is reproduced verbatim. All spelling, grammatical, and punctuation errors were present in the original document.

Photostatic copy of classified section of Washington Post newspaper dated November 9, 1973 in which Mrs. Sullivan's ad appears as follows:

> "Alex. Empl. Yng. Man; on bus line,
> residential sec.
> 836-2126"

Buffington in which he confesses in detail to having stolen money from woman in Alexandria, Virginia on November 12, 1973).

Admits letter is in his own handwriting (T.64) and admitted into evidence at trial. (T.64).

July 1974 - Defendant confesses to crime in Alexandria, Virginia and Government learns of crime for first time.

July 1974 - Defendant is convicted of murder in the 1st degree and sentenced to life imprisonment.

Jan. 1975 – Mark Kolman, the prosecutor in the Smith murder trial leaves Baltimore City State's Attorney's Office.

Feb. 1976 – Murder conviction reversed.

May 1976 – No one individual had any actual notice and entire matter remained in dormant state until …

July 1978 – When Carole Buffington alerted our office by telephone that Smith was due for release shortly.

August 1978 – Sam Brave, Assistant State's Attorney and Detective Frank Perkowski assemble all pertinent information and meet with Alexandria, Virginia prosecutors

September 1978 – State's Attorney's Office, Baltimore City formally requests institution of criminal proceedings in Alexandria, Virginia.

APPENDIX C:
VICTIM IMPACT STATEMENTS FROM SACRAMENTO, CALIFORNIA

According to the victim of count one, she indicated that she felt that defendant should be required to repay all of the victim in full for their losses and serve time in State Prison. She indicated that most of the defendant's victims were senior citizens who were attempting to supplement their income by renting a room in their homes.

According to the victim count two, she indicated that she has no compassion for the defendant. She stated that she could not have taken advantage of her at any worse time in her life financially and emotionally. She had just started a new job and had received her first paycheck when she loaned the defendant $380.00 leaving 'her with $20.00 in her savings account. After she realized that she had "been had" by the defendant, she "completely went downhill emotionally." She was hospitalized for four days for a serious kidney infection, followed by three months in therapy and anti-depressant medication.

According to the victim of count three, she has only feelings of "contempt" for the defendant. The victim of count four, informed this officer that she could not afford the loss sustained as a result of the defendant's actions, and further, indicated that the defendant threatened her and told her to keep her mouth shut or else. The victim of count five indicated that she had no compassion for the defendant and felt that he should be made to make restitution to his victims. She indicated that as a result of the defendant's actions, she has suffered a great deal of mental anguish and feels that he should not be allowed on the streets, but rather that he should be "put away for good."

According to victim of information #59427, she indicated that while at the defendant's residence, and during the course of their struggle, she lost a diamond ring valued at approximately $2,000.00. According the victim, when the defendant informed her that he was going to kill her, she felt certain that he meant to do so. She feels that the defendant is a "pathological liar" and since her ordeal, she does not trust any men and keeps her doors barricaded at night. She has stated that as a result of the defendant's actions, she has suffered not only a financial loss as a result of the loss of her diamond ring, but also has suffered a "great deal of mental anguish."

www.ingramcontent.com/pod-product-compliance
Lightning Source LLC
Chambersburg PA
CBHW051802040426
42446CB00007B/477